CORONA CRISIS

CORONA CRISIS

PLAGUES, PANDEMICS, AND THE COMING APOCALYPSE

MARK HITCHCOCK

W PUBLISHING GROUP

AN IMPRINT OF THOMAS NELSON

Published in Nashville, Tennessee, by W Publishing Group, an imprint of Thomas Nelson.

Published in association with William K. Jensen Literary Agency, 119 Bampton Court, Eugene, Oregon 97404.

Thomas Nelson titles may be purchased in bulk for educational, business, fundraising, or sales promotional use. For information, please email SpecialMarkets@ThomasNelson.com.

Unless otherwise noted, scripture quotations taken from The Holy Bible, New International Version®, NIV®. Copyright © 1973, 1978, 1984, 2011 by Biblica, Inc.® Used by permission of Zondervan. All rights reserved worldwide. www.Zondervan. com. The "NIV" and "New International Version" are trademarks registered in the United States Patent and Trademark Office by Biblica, Inc.®

Scripture quotations marked NASB are taken from the New American Standard Bible® (NASB). Copyright © 1960, 1962, 1963, 1968, 1971, 1972, 1973, 1975, 1977, 1995 by The Lockman Foundation. Used by permission. www.lockman.org

Scripture quotations marked NKJV are taken from the New King James Version®. Copyright © 1982 by Thomas Nelson. Used by permission. All rights reserved.

ISBN 978-0-7852-4003-7 (eBook)

Library of Congress Control Number: 2020936438

ISBN 978-0-7852-4002-0

20 21 22 23 24   LSC   10 9 8 7 6 5 4 3 2 1

CONTENTS

To my grandson Reed Wilson Hitchcock

*I thank God daily for adding your smile
and sunlight to our family. Just thinking
about you makes me smile. I can't remember
what we did without you. I look forward
to watching you grow up and, by God's
grace, come to know and love Jesus.*

Are we approaching those days of which the Bible speaks? Are the events of our time meant to warn us of even greater disasters—disasters predicted by the Bible that will be harbingers of Christ's coming judgment and rule?

—BILLY GRAHAM, *STORM WARNING*

PREFACE

What in the World Is Going On?

*From now on, it can be said that plague
was the concern of all of us.*

—Albert Camus, *The Plague*

On February 29, 2020, my wife, Cheryl, and I left our home in Edmond, Oklahoma, for a thirteen-day trip to Israel. We could never have imagined how drastically the world would change by the time we returned.

Our flight from the States to Tel Aviv connected in Frankfurt, Germany. The airport there was eerily quiet and empty, but when we arrived in Israel, the place was bustling with excited tourists. Everything seemed normal. Tour groups from China and South Korea were prohibited, but groups from the United States were abundant.

Cheryl and I were joined a few days after our arrival by the rest of the tour group we were leading. COVID-19, a new form of coronavirus, was in the news when we departed, but its potential impact on the US was still being watched and weighed. There was a looming sense of concern and uncertainty; however, the virus had not yet erupted into a full pandemic, as the hot zones were still China and South Korea.

Fast-forward several days. The coronavirus had quickly mushroomed in Europe, especially Italy. Israel had acted quickly and decisively, barring all arriving flights from Europe and other affected areas.

A few days before we were set to return to the States, everyone's phones began blowing up. An NBA player for the Utah Jazz, which was scheduled to play the Oklahoma City Thunder, was diagnosed with the virus. The game in Oklahoma City at the Chesapeake Arena was canceled just before tip-off.

The virus had hit home.

From there the dominoes began to fall. President Trump canceled all flights to the US from Europe, with the exception of the United Kingdom and Ireland (though they would be included later). Everyone in our tour group with a connection in Europe had to reschedule their flights. Frustrating calls to overwhelmed airlines dragged on for several hours. Relatives and friends back home were concerned about our safe and speedy return. My wife was barraged with text messages from anxious loved ones.

Our tour group was one of the final ones to exit Israel. No more groups were allowed to leave after we did. During our final day of touring in Jerusalem, the streets were virtually empty. Vendors were absent. Shops were closed. Israel was preparing to hunker down for the long haul.

When we finally arrived back home, after only two weeks away, it felt as if we had returned to a different country—a strange new world. It's difficult to describe how we felt, but it was profoundly surreal. Our time in Israel had distanced and insulated us from the surging chaos and upheaval back home. Cable news shows in the US had coronavirus coverage 24/7. Store shelves were ransacked. Bottled water was scarce. Toilet paper was nowhere to be found. Quarantines were mandated. Cruise ships were stranded. Events of all kinds were canceled. The NBA, NHL, and MLB all suspended their seasons. High school and college sports seasons were ended. The NCAA's March Madness was scratched. Schools closed. Restaurants suspended dine-in service. Bars shut down. Pastors preached to empty pews and chairs as church services were broadcast via livestream. Streets emptied.

Gatherings of more than ten people were forbidden. Global stock markets collapsed.

Just as we returned, President Trump, surrounded by an august group of health experts, rallied the American people to significantly limit social interaction for fifteen days to break the back of the virus and flatten the curve of infection. The lockdown dragged on. Uncertainty and panic spread.

The world was changed forever.

SIGNPOST ON THE ROAD TO ARMAGEDDON

As I am writing, we are still in the midst of the crisis, and the main concerns of all Americans and citizens of other affected nations are the physical health and safety of our families, neighbors, and friends. That's priority one. But people are also gravely concerned about their jobs and the economy. We all hope and pray that the hit on the economy won't crater into a deep recession or even a depression. Physical and fiscal health are the two overriding concerns, and they are deeply interconnected. Yet there's another issue that's lurking in the minds of many people, a lingering concern that what we're seeing may be a portent of things to come—a harbinger of the end of days.

As my wife and I were standing in line in Tel Aviv to board our delayed flight to Newark, New Jersey, two young men were standing just in front of us. I struck up a conversation with them, and at one point one of them looked at my wife and me with a bewildered expression on his face and said, "I don't know what in the world is going on. I think the world is about to end."

I was surprised by his unexpected comment, but I told him, "This isn't the end of the world, but I do believe Jesus could come at any time, and we need to make sure we know Him and that we're ready." He looked back at me with a blank stare, clearly having no idea how these two thoughts were connected, and then turned back to talk with his friend.

That young man's question, in one form or another, has probably been on the minds of many people in recent days. Empty streets, closed malls and shopping centers, people holed up in their homes "sheltering in place" . . . these days certainly have an apocalyptic feel. Apocalypse is in the air. While many people may not want to say it aloud, they're secretly wondering if the COVID-19 pandemic is an omen of the end—a sign or signal of what's to come. Another signpost on the road to Armageddon. Even the *Washington Post* ran an article on March 18, 2020, about what Christians who study the end of the world were saying about the corona crisis.[1]

ECHOES OF THE END

Simply stated, that's what this book is about: the intersection of plagues and the coming Apocalypse. We'll concentrate on the rise of deadly viruses in the last few decades and consider what role pandemics will play in the end of days. Of course, the current focus is on COVID-19, but the coronavirus is only one of a long chain of outbreaks the world has experienced in recent times. We'll highlight some of these other plagues in chapter 3.

Zeroing in on the coronavirus outbreak, Dr. Albert Mohler, president of Southern Baptist Theological Seminary, said,

> But Christians looking to this news and of course looking with concern also have to look, recognizing that we are hearing echoes of what we find in Scripture. For example, in the Gospel of Luke 21:11 where Jesus says, "There will be earthquakes and in various places, plagues and famines and there will be terrors and great signs from heaven."[2]

Dr. Mohler is spot on. The coronavirus plague echoes what we find in Scripture. It foreshadows what lies ahead, which raises many compelling questions that deserve clear answers.

- Are current events part of a larger drama scripted long ago?
- Does the Bible predict the rise of pestilence and plagues in the end times?
- Is the coronavirus prophesied in the Bible?
- Is the coronavirus the judgment of God?
- How bad will it get?
- Are we living in the end times?
- Where is the current crisis headed?
- How should we respond in light of the corona crisis?

Answers to these questions won't tell us everything we want to know about the future or pinpoint the time of Jesus' coming, but they will place the current crisis into a scriptural framework that helps us understand what lies ahead and teaches us how to live until Jesus comes again. In all this, we need to remember that God told us about the future not to scare us but to prepare us, not to make us anxious but to make us aware.

So join me as we unpack today's ominous headlines and connect the dots with ancient prophecies in the pages of Scripture. Together, let's discover what in the world is going on and make sure we're aware and prepared.

CHAPTER 1

CORONA FEVER

*We're waking up to our new
reality. . . . This will be the thing
this generation remembers.*

—Amy Acton, Ohio Department
of Health Director

*"People will faint from terror,
apprehensive of what is
coming on the world."*

—Jesus, Luke 21:26

N one of us, in our wildest dreams, ever thought we
would spend so many days and weeks of our lives

thinking about a microscopic virus. It's not something we like to think about or want to think about. Now or ever! Yet our lives have been consumed by novel coronavirus disease 2019 (COVID-19).[1] We're bombarded and barraged with it every waking moment. It's 24/7. We've heard from doctors, epidemiologists, politicians, financial experts, and political pundits nonstop. We've seen charts and graphics predicting how bad it's going to get. No one living through these times will ever forget 2020 and COVID-19.

The coronavirus has turned the entire world upside down. It's a classic "black swan" event.[2] We're witnessing worldwide upheaval. The headlines tell the story:

"APOCALYPSE NOW: HERE'S HOW
AMERICANS THINK IT WILL ALL END"
YOUGOV.COM, MARCH 18, 2020

"CORONAVIRUS WILL CHANGE THE
WORLD PERMANENTLY. HERE'S HOW."
POLITICO, MARCH 19, 2020

"WHY DO SOME CHRISTIANS
BELIEVE CORONAVIRUS IS AN
APOCALYPTIC PROPHECY?"
THE JERUSALEM POST, MARCH 26, 2020

"Empty Streets and Sights as
Major Cities Lock Down"
BBC News, March 29, 2020

"Trump Acknowledges That Deaths in
the US Could Reach 100,000 or More"
Associated Press, March 29, 2020

"Over 3,000 People Have Died in US from
Coronavirus, Surpassing 9/11 Death Toll"
New York Post, March 31, 2020

"US Jobless Claims Hit Record 6.6
Million as COVID-19 Ravages Economy"
The Guardian, April 2, 2020

Never in my lifetime have I sensed so much anxiety and unrest. It's palpable. Never, other than briefly after the 9/11 terrorist attacks, has nearly every conversation been dominated by one topic. Conversations are centered around coronavirus and its consequences and impact on daily life.

We're navigating uncharted waters. These are turbulent, unparalleled, unprecedented times. There's a daily Niagara Falls of unnerving news. It's easy to get overwhelmed. Isolation is exacting its grinding toll.

VIRAL SPIRAL

On New Year's Eve 2019, health officials from China alerted the World Health Organization of a new form of pneumonia in the city of Wuhan, a megacity in the Central China region.

A few days later, health officials announced they had identified a new strain of virus from the coronavirus family. It was labeled "2019-nCoV," more commonly known as COVID-19 or the coronavirus.

The number of cases exploded in China, and then Italy and Spain were hit hard. The first COVID-19 death in the United States was on February 29, 2020. The US eventually surpassed China as the country with the most confirmed cases. New York City became the global epicenter.

Coronavirus hit the elderly population hardest along with those with underlying medical issues. Experts maintain we will never know the full extent of the pandemic since some people have no discernible symptoms. But one thing we do know is that coronavirus changed the world. That's not an overstatement or exaggeration, since COVID-19 spread to almost every nation on the planet and reached into every corner and crevice of our lives. Our schedules, schools, social contacts, hygiene, work, psyches, and—for many people—interest in spiritual things. Shaking hands or hugging became taboo. We had to keep our distance from everyone.

Like thousands of other pastors, I preached for weeks to an empty sanctuary as our services were live-streamed to our people in their homes. It was not ideal, but it was a great reminder to us all that the church is not the building or the gathering but the people who are part of Christ's body. Still, preaching to an empty room on Good Friday and Easter Sunday was an experience I will never forget.

Even our vocabulary changed in a short period of time. New words and phrases we've all heard and learned have become part of our everyday conversation: self-isolation, self-quarantine, shelter in place, social distance, community spread, coronavirus, n95 mask, COVID-19, super-spreader, flatten the curve, and pandemic. There's no doubt the word of the year for 2020 will be *coronavirus*. It may be the word of the new decade.

It seems like we've all been suddenly written into the script of a movie about the spread of a mysterious apocalyptic virus—think *Outbreak* (1995) or *Contagion* (2011), the latter of which became one of the most-watched movies during the corona crisis. Or it seems like we're part of the nightmarish plot of one of the spate of movies that portrays a dystopian future after a pandemic, war, or ecological disaster: *World War Z*,

28 Days Later, *The Walking Dead*, or *The Last of Us*. Strange times indeed.

India went on lockdown, quarantining one-sixth of the world's population. Italy shut down as tight as a condemned building. While I'm writing, 90 percent of the US population is under some level of lockdown or stay-at-home / shelter-in-place order. Storefronts are plastered with signs stating "Closed Until Further Notice." Streets are eerily empty. High-rise office buildings are vacant. Playgrounds are silent. Tent hospitals have sprung up in New York City's Central Park. Floating naval hospitals are anchored off the coasts of New York City and Los Angeles. Writing for *The Atlantic*, Ed Yong said,

> Three months ago, no one knew that SARS-CoV-2 existed. Now the virus has spread to almost every country. . . . It has crashed economies and broken health-care systems, filled hospitals and emptied public spaces. It has separated people from their workplaces and their friends. It has disrupted modern society on a scale that most living people have never witnessed. Soon, most everyone in the United States will know someone who has been infected. Like World War II or the 9/11 attacks, this pandemic has already imprinted itself upon the nation's psyche.[3]

On top of all the other personal anxiety, financial markets plummeted. The US stock market logged its worst first quarter in 124 years. Experts called it a major financial reset. The largest economic relief and stimulus package in history was passed by Congress and signed by President Donald Trump. More rounds are expected.

Global travel lurched to a standstill. Unemployment could quickly surge to near 1930s levels. There's no doubt that the world is being battered psychologically, socially, physically, and financially. But COVID-19 has had another powerful effect, reaching into our collective psyche prophetically and apocalyptically. Everywhere you look, more and more people are wondering if, in addition to all the other impact, coronavirus signals the beginning of the end. With the sudden surge of COVID-19, it's not uncommon to hear the words *apocalyptic*, *doomsday*, or *last days* used to describe what's happening. We often use those words loosely, but in this case many people seem to be using them in a more literal sense. With the entire world on edge, many are asking searching questions:

- Is this the beginning of the great tribulation?
- Will coronavirus lead to the end of the world as we know it?

- Is it a sign of Christ's soon return?
- Are these the "beginning of birth pains," as Jesus predicted in Matthew 24:8?

Opinions on this topic are flying all over the internet and social media in every conceivable direction as people struggle to make sense of what's happening.[4]

THE HARBINGER

Without doubt, the global spread of coronavirus has a strange, apocalyptic feel. In March 2020, as my wife and I were at Armageddon, the ancient ruins of Megiddo in Israel, leading a tour group from our church, the corona crisis was ramping up. The site at Armageddon is fascinating, and it felt surreal being there as a global pandemic was tightening its grip on the globe. We were there on a beautiful, clear day, which was great since the ancient site of Megiddo overlooks the expansive Jezreel Valley, or Valley of Armageddon. As always, I presented a teaching on the final great military conflict from Revelation 16 and 19.

After we returned to the States, I read that even Armageddon was on lockdown in light of the COVID-19 outbreak.[5] I couldn't help but think that things have gotten pretty bad when Armageddon is off limits and locked down. The site at Armageddon may be closed, but the events that will lead to that final great conflagration are ramping up. Our world is well down the road that leads to Armageddon.

Even the *New York Times* has taken note of the apocalyptic character of the times as natural disasters seem to be escalating:

> For people of many faiths, and even none at all, it can feel lately like the end of the world is near. Not only is there a plague, but hundreds of billions of locusts are swarming East Africa. Wildfires have ravaged Australia, killing an untold number of animals. A recent earthquake in Utah even shook the Salt Lake Temple to the top of its iconic spire, causing the golden trumpet to fall from the angel Moroni's right hand.[6]

Many are pointing to these events as flashing signs of the end. The shaking of the foundations.

Pastor and prophecy expert David Jeremiah, who is not given to sensationalism or hyperbole, called the COVID-19 pandemic "the most apocalyptic thing that has ever happened to us."[7] The American people seem to share that sentiment.

In a poll of likely voters in the United States,

conducted by the nationally recognized McLaughlin & Associates, "A stunning 44.3% of poll respondents said they believe the coronavirus and resulting economic meltdown is a 'wake-up call for us to turn back to faith in God,' signs of 'coming judgment,' or both."[8] That's astounding. Additionally, 29 percent of those polled believe the corona crisis suggests that "we are living in what the Bible calls the 'last days.'"[9] This poll is not a fringe finding or outlier. It's an accurate reading of the nation's prophetic pulse.

I heard a story years ago about a man who visited the Upper Peninsula of Michigan with a friend. Stunned by the solitary beauty, he commented, "This looks like the end of the world." His friend replied, "It's not the end of the world, but I think you can see it from here."

That's how many people are feeling today. Even people with little or no religious belief or conviction have an uneasy, foreboding sense that doomsday is approaching. That we can see the end from here.

They may be right. Scripture predicts events that will shake and shatter the foundations of society in the end times. The Bible urges us to pay attention to the crises in our world that will lead to the final events that must take place before Jesus returns. Among those future crises or catastrophes is pestilence, plagues, and pandemics—like coronavirus.

2020 VISION

It's well known that President Ronald Reagan was extremely nearsighted. Reagan's eyesight was so bad that it affected his military service in World War II, keeping him from combat duty. For many years he wore glasses and later contact lenses. As he aged, he still needed correction for his nearsightedness but also needed help to see up close. He wore a lens to correct nearsightedness on his right eye and a lens for farsightedness on his left eye. So he would read his speeches with his right eye and look out at the audience with his left eye. President Reagan was a man focused on the near and the far.[10]

In these unprecedented times, we want the same to be true of us. We need double vision. We need to be ever watchful, simultaneously looking with one eye toward the end times and the other on the meantime. We need to be focused on what's up close: Our health. Our families. Our communities. Ministering to those around us who are in need. But if all we do is focus on what's nearby, we can become anxious and alarmed. We need to keep an eye on the sky. As pastor Philip De Courcy observed,

> It's easy to become alarmed if we remain nearsighted. After all . . . famine and natural disasters abound, wars and rumors of wars fill our conversation,

economic globalism is on the rise. . . . We must not be nearsighted alone, we must also be farsighted. To survive and thrive in a world gone mad, we as Christians must begin with the end, we must constantly and confidently keep an eye on the horizon as we look for the second coming of Christ in the clouds with power and glory.[11]

We need both eyes. It's easy to get out of balance. I like this thought from author Max Lucado, calling us to strike a proper balance: "Some Christians are so obsessed with the last days that they are oblivious to these days. Others are just the opposite. They'll tell you Jesus is coming. But they live like he never will. One is too panicky, the other too patient. Isn't there a balance?"[12] There is, and we would do well to find it, especially in these challenging times. We need to keep our vision balanced and focused.

We will try to do that throughout this book. We want to look at what's ahead because that's the focus of this book, but we also want to think about how to live today in light of what's coming. Interestingly, as we look at current events and headlines, the near and far seem to be moving closer together every day—even appearing to be on the verge of merging.

With that in mind, it's not my desire to stir up needless anxiety or arouse groundless fears; rather,

I hope to deal with questions people everywhere are asking and to connect some prophetic dots by turning to Scripture for answers. I invite you to come with me as we discover the answers God has given us in His inspired Word, the Bible.

CHAPTER 2

THE TIMES OF
THE SIGNS

*The Bible gives . . . clear indications that
will alert us to Christ's soon return. And
here's what I find so fascinating: There are
more of those signs in closer proximity to
one another than I have ever seen before.*

—GREG LAURIE, *SIGNS OF THE TIMES*

Every Tuesday during the school year, I drive from
our house in the Oklahoma City area down I-35 to
Dallas Theological Seminary, where I have the privilege
of teaching. I've driven that stretch of road hundreds of

times. I know the road extremely well. Maybe too well. Many of the signs along the highway are very familiar. I use the signs as markers to know where I am and to determine how much longer it will be until I arrive.

Some of the highway signs are informational, like "Exit 51" or "Dallas 180 Miles." Other familiar signs are invitational, such as "Welcome to Texas" or "Best Barbecue in Oklahoma 5 Miles." However, the signs that grab my attention, no matter how many times I make the drive, are the new warning signs: "Left Lane Closed Ahead," "Merge Now," or "Road Work Next 5 Miles." Some of these warning signs have flashing lights. You can't miss them.

One other thing about the signs on I-35 is that the closer I get to the seminary campus, the greater the number of signs I see. As I approach Dallas and then get into the city, signs are everywhere. You can't miss them. They increase in number and are closer together.

All the signs we encounter along any road, whether informational, invitational, or instructional, are designed with one simple goal in mind: to help us get safely from where we are to our final destination.

In a similar way, God has posted signs that highlight where we are today and where we're going. These signs point to future events. We find these signs of the times in God's Word, the Bible.[1] These signs tell us what we can expect on the road ahead. Some of these signs are more familiar. They've been in place for a while. Many are new. Some of them have flashing lights. Also, just as the signposts increase the closer I get to Dallas, signs of the times are increasing the closer we get to the end of the age.

People everywhere sense it. It's palpable. The signs are multiplying. They're lining up. Global events are tilting and trending toward the end of days. Turmoil in the Middle East, the rise of Russia and Iran, the threat of nuclear proliferation, globalism, natural disasters, and now the surging coronavirus pandemic and panic.

THE SAVIOR AND SIGNS

Of course, none of this takes the Lord by surprise. God is never caught off guard. In fact, Jesus Himself spoke frequently about signs of the times. This might amaze some people. In one encounter with the religious leaders of His day, Jesus rebuked them for blindly refusing to see the signs swirling around them.

> The Pharisees and Sadducees came to Jesus and tested him by asking him to show them a sign from heaven.

> He replied, "When evening comes, you say, 'It will be fair weather, for the sky is red,' and in the morning, 'Today it will be stormy, for the sky is red and overcast.' You know how to interpret the appearance of the sky, but you cannot interpret the signs of the times." (Matthew 16:1–3)

Jesus was saying these religious leaders were master meteorologists, but they were incompetent interpreters of the signs of the times. They totally missed the clear signs of His first coming. They were blind to all the obvious signs that identified Him as the Messiah. In the same way, many today are blind to the signs of His second coming, which He's meticulously laid out for us. In Matthew 24:4–28, Jesus gave a long list of signs that will telegraph His return. In Luke 21:25, He spoke of dramatic cosmic signs.

Jesus called His followers to discern the signs of the times.

DISCERNING THE SIGNS

As we observe and evaluate current events and world headlines in relation to signs of the times, we need to set up a few important guardrails to make sure we stay on the road and don't drive into the ditch. Let me suggest four principal parameters.

1. Seriousness, Not Sensationalism

First, we must shun a sensationalistic approach to current events and world headlines. Any time there's a crisis or natural disaster such as COVID-19, a chorus of voices immediately begin to announce the advent of the Antichrist and imminent arrival of the Apocalypse. Wild speculation often spreads faster than the virus. Some prophecy teachers cry wolf about every event, no matter how insignificant, so often that thinking people turn off the noise and don't listen to them anymore. For sensationalists, every earthquake, war, terrorist attack, disease, crime spree, famine, hurricane, or tsunami is a flashing neon sign pointing to the end. The problem with this kind of news headline exegesis is that if everything is a sign, then nothing is a sign. We can't manufacture every current event into a sign of the times. Doing so dilutes the serious impact and force of true, discernible signs outlined in Scripture.

2. Scripture First, Not Headlines

Second, current events, headlines, and world news must be assessed in light of the Bible, not the other way around. We must remember the Bible is the final source about signs of the times. We get all our information about end-time events from God's Word. It's the only reliable authority about the future. The Bible is a book of prophecy. Within its sixty-six books we find a staggering one thousand prophecies, penned over a period of fifteen hundred years by forty different human authors. About half of those prophecies have already been fulfilled, so we know the rest will one day be fulfilled as well. The Bible's track record is pristine. It's flawless. We can put it to the test. You can trust the prophecies found in Scripture.

Danger arises when people fall prey to the temptation to find some sensational event in the headlines and then go searching for some obscure scripture, often wrenched out of context, to support what the news is reporting. That's reckless and irresponsible. We must consult the biblical blueprint for the end times first, and then responsibly look at world events and their correspondence, if any, to Scripture. The Bible is our infallible prophetic template.

Of course, the most egregious, reckless form of prophetic pandering is setting dates for specific end-time events to occur. Every so often someone comes along and sets a date for the return of Christ. They do this despite Jesus saying during His time on earth that even He didn't know the time of His second coming.

"But about that day or hour no one knows, not even the angels in heaven, nor the Son, but only the Father" (Matthew 24:36). That means those who allege to know the date of Christ's return are claiming to know something even Jesus didn't know. That's pretty bold . . . and extremely foolish. When someone sets a specific date for the second coming, I know I can always rule out that date, since Jesus said, "So you also must be ready, because the Son of Man will come at an hour when you do not expect him" (v. 44).

Date setters are upsetters and must be ignored and rejected.

3. Second Coming, Not the Rapture

A third important principle for signs of the times is to remember that they relate directly to Jesus' second coming back to earth, not the rapture. Understanding this point requires us to fill in a little bit of end-time background and chronology and define a few important prophetic terms.

Let's begin with the rapture since it's the next event on God's prophetic calendar. The rapture is an imminent event, meaning it could happen at any moment. We know it will happen, but we can't know when it will happen. It's an event without a sign. In other words, nothing needs to transpire before the rapture takes place. It will happen in a split second, in the time it takes to blink your eye. At the rapture, believers—both living and dead—will be taken up to meet Jesus in the air and accompany Him back to heaven. The bodies of the dead will be resurrected to rejoin their perfected spirits. The living will be raptured—that is, they will be caught up to heaven and transformed without ever tasting death.

Three main New Testament texts describe this event that will shock the world:

> "Do not let your hearts be troubled. You believe in God; believe also in me. My Father's house has many rooms; if that were not so, would I have told you that I am going there to prepare a place for you? And if I go and prepare a place for you, I will come back and take you to be with me that you also may be where I am." (John 14:1–3)

> Listen, I tell you a mystery: We will not all sleep, but we will all be changed—in a flash, in the twinkling of an eye, at the last trumpet. For the trumpet will sound, the dead will be raised imperishable, and we will be changed. For the perishable must clothe itself with the imperishable, and the mortal with immortality. (1 Corinthians 15:51–53)

> For the Lord himself will come down from heaven, with a loud command, with the voice of the archangel and with the trumpet call of God, and the dead in Christ will rise first. After that, we who are still alive and are left will be caught up together with them in the clouds to meet the Lord in the air. And so we will be with the Lord forever. Therefore encourage one another with these words. (1 Thessalonians 4:16–18)

The rapture will be God's rescue operation. The rapture will deliver living believers from the horror of the next event on the prophetic calendar, the tribulation period (1 Thessalonians 1:9–10; Revelation 3:10–11). That means believers today are looking for Christ, not the Antichrist. The tribulation period will last seven years and will commence with a seven-year peace treaty forged by the Antichrist with Israel (Daniel 9:27). The ongoing, seemingly endless Middle East peace process is a foreshadow of this future accord.

The seven years of tribulation will be hell on earth. The Lord will pour out His judgment upon the earth in three successive waves vividly unveiled in Revelation 6–18. Yet, in His mercy and grace, God will use those dark, terrible days to save an innumerable host of people (7:9–17).

The last half of the tribulation, or final three and a half years, is often called the "great tribulation" (Matthew 24:21 NASB). During this brief span, the Antichrist will seize control, ruling the world politically, economically, and religiously. The entire world will be forced to give total allegiance to him—or suffer persecution and death (Revelation 13:1–18). He will employ a distinguishing mark to signify loyalty and allegiance to him: the number 666. It's called the mark of the Beast.

The great tribulation will end with the battle of Armageddon. All the armies of the earth will gather in the land of Israel for a final showdown. Revelation graphically describes earth's final death struggle:

> The sixth angel poured out his bowl on the great river Euphrates, and its water was dried up to prepare the way for the kings from the East. Then I saw three impure spirits that looked like frogs; they came out of the mouth of the dragon, out of the mouth of the beast and out of the mouth of the false prophet. They are demonic spirits that perform signs, and they go out to the kings of the whole world, to gather them for the battle on the great day of God Almighty. . . .
> Then they gathered the kings together to the place that in Hebrew is called Armageddon. (16:12–14, 16)

The battle of Armageddon will suddenly be interrupted by the climactic event of human history—the literal, physical, visible, glorious return of Jesus Christ to planet Earth. Jesus will return accompanied by those He raptured to heaven seven years earlier. He will destroy the gathered armies and cast the Antichrist and his evil associate, the false prophet, into the lake of fire. The glorious revelation of Jesus is described in Revelation 19:

> I saw heaven standing open and there before me was a white horse, whose rider is called Faithful and True. With justice he judges and wages war. His eyes are like blazing fire, and on his head are many crowns. He has a name written on him that no one knows but he himself. He is dressed in a robe dipped in blood, and his name is the Word of God. The armies of heaven were following him, riding on white horses and dressed in fine linen, white and clean. Coming out of his mouth is a sharp sword with which to strike down the nations. "He will rule them with an iron scepter." He treads the winepress of the fury of the wrath of God Almighty. On his robe and on his thigh he has this name written: KING OF KINGS AND LORD OF LORDS. (vv. 11–16)

After His return, Jesus will establish His kingdom of peace and prosperity and rule the world for one thousand years, followed by the creation of the new heaven and new earth (Revelation 20–22).

You have to admit, that's quite an outlook.

The central point I want to emphasize, however, is that the rapture and the return are two distinct phases or stages of the second coming of Christ, separated by the tribulation. Jesus will come *for* His saints at the rapture, before the tribulation, and then come *with* His saints at the end of the tribulation. This chart highlights some of the more salient differences between these two phases of Jesus' coming:

The Rapture	The Return
Christ comes in the air (1 Thess. 4:16–17)	Christ comes to earth (Zech. 14:4)
Christ comes for His saints (1 Thess. 4:16–17)	Christ comes with His saints (1 Thess. 3:13; Jude 14)
Movement from earth to heaven	Movement from heaven to earth

No signs—it is imminent	Portended by many signs (Matt. 24:4–29)
Time of blessing and comfort (1 Thess. 4:18)	Time of destruction and judgment (2 Thess. 2:8–12)
Involves believers only (John 14:1–3; 1 Cor. 15:51–55; 1 Thess. 4:13–18)	Involves Israel and Gentile nations (Matt. 24–25)
Will occur in the blink of an eye, to only Christ's own (1 Cor. 15:51–52)	Will be visible to the entire world (Matt. 24:27; Rev. 1:7)

The reason I'm underscoring this distinction is that the signs of Christ's coming set forth in the New Testament deal with the return of Jesus to earth, not the rapture. None of the passages that describe the rapture include any mention of signs. There are no signs for the rapture. It's a signless event. So, what is the relationship, if any, of signs to the rapture? Do signs relate to the rapture in any way? I believe they do.

Let me explain by using a simple illustration involving Christmas and Thanksgiving. When it comes to signs, the return of Christ is like Christmas. There are all kinds of signs that Christmas is drawing near. Christmas music in the mall. Decorations everywhere. Nativity scenes. Christmas lights on shopping centers and homes. Santa everywhere. Hallmark Christmas movies 24/7. Signs of Christmas abound.

The rapture, on the other hand, is like Thanksgiving. There are no specific signs for Thanksgiving, unless you're a turkey. Nevertheless, if it's late summer or early fall, and you begin to see signs for Christmas all around but Thanksgiving has not arrived, you know it must be near. In the same way, as we see the proliferation of signs for the return and the rapture has not yet happened, we can expect that the rapture is near. In that way, escalating signs we see today, such as globalism, world focus on the Middle East, spiritual deception, and even the coronavirus pandemic serve as a kind of prophetic overlap that points toward the rapture.

4. Stage Setting, Not Fulfillment

One final parameter for signs of the times is that most of what we see today is not the direct fulfillment of end-time prophecy but rather a foreshadow of what will come after God's people have been raptured to heaven.

The main prophecy that I believe is being fulfilled today is the regathering of the Jewish people to their ancient homeland. This regathering is predicted by the Old Testament prophets many times (see Ezekiel 37, for example). The modern state of Israel was founded, against all odds, in 1948. That event was a prophetic watershed. Israel is God's timepiece—His prophetic, end-time alarm clock. Israel is often called the "super-sign" of the end times because so many other prophecies are dependent upon it. Israel is the epicenter of God's prophetic program. If you want to know where we are on God's prophetic calendar, look at Israel. And when we look at Israel, all signs point to a converging crisis.

Other than Israel, the rest of the prophetically significant events we see today, such as COVID-19, are not fulfillments of specific prophecies but are setting the stage for events that will begin to unfold after the rapture. Today, God is preparing the world for what's coming. God is in control. He is the director who is setting the world's stage for the coming drama of the tribulation. Authors Thomas Ice and Timothy Demy said, "Just as many people set their clothes out the night before they wear them the following day, so in the same sense is God preparing the world for the certain fulfillment of prophecy in a future time."[2]

CORONAVIRUS AND CONVERGENCE

I believe coronavirus is part of the stage setting for the end times. In that sense, it's a sign that points beyond itself to future events. For example, coronavirus is revealing the interconnectedness of the modern world as well as accelerating it. Author Bryan Walsh spotlighted this connection:

> As Covid-19 is painfully demonstrating, our inter-connected global economy both helps spread new infectious diseases—and, with its long supply chains, is uniquely vulnerable to the disruption that they can cause. The ability to get to nearly any spot in the world in 20 hours or fewer, and pack a virus along with our carry-on luggage, allows new diseases to emerge and to grow when they might have died out in the past.[3]

Rapid means of world travel provide the perfect environment for plagues to spread quickly around the world. This points toward the pandemics that will surge in the end times.

COVID-19 is also speeding the rise of globalism. The pandemic intersects with the drive toward a one-world economy and government that will fall under the rule of a global strongman, the final Antichrist (Revelation 13:1–18). The global framework that must be in place for the Antichrist to rise to power is gaining momentum in the face of the pandemic.

Gordon Brown, a former prime minister of the United Kingdom, "has urged world leaders to create a temporary form of global government to tackle the twin medical and economic crises caused by the Covid-19 pandemic." He said he believes countries cannot deal with this effectively on their own but that there should be some sort of coordinated effort to fight it. Brown added, "We need some sort of working executive."[4] This approach to combatting COVID-19 is underscoring and expediting the movement toward globalism—supporting what the Bible says will happen in the end times.

POSITIVE SIGNS

The road to the Apocalypse is lined with signs. If we're honest, some of them are frightening and foreboding, such as a pandemic plague. Still, it's important for us to keep our eyes on the signs, even when we'd rather look away. We ignore them at our peril.

Yet, at the same time, we can't allow ourselves to get enamored with the signs. Any driver who focuses all his or her attention on the signs is headed for trouble. Signs are important, but they aren't all-important. Their only value is to point to something beyond themselves. Signs show us the way and lead us from where we are to where we want to be. And the ultimate place we want to be is with Jesus in His kingdom. The signs lead us home.

My friend and fellow pastor Philip De Courcy said it well:

> All this bad news must in a way be viewed as good news because the signs of our times are pointing to the signs of the end time and the recapture of Earth by Heaven at the return of Christ. The Bible tells us things will get worse before they get better. . . . We must not be nearsighted alone, we must also be far-sighted. To survive and thrive in a world gone mad, we as Christians must begin with the end, we must constantly and confidently keep an eye on the horizon as we look forward to the second coming of Christ in the clouds with power and glory.[5]

The signs are all pointing in the same direction: the coming of Jesus and a world recaptured by heaven. Take comfort—the best is yet to come.

CHAPTER 3

PLAGUES—PAST AND PRESENT

Jesus also taught his disciples that
we are to understand that the end is
always near . . . that at no time are
we ever far from the apocalypse.
—DR. ALBERT MOHLER, *THE BRIEFING*

There are some words that get a strong reaction from almost everyone. Words that strike fear in our hearts just by hearing them spoken. I'm sure you can think of some, but here are a few that come to mind: *terrorism, cancer, tornado* (I'm from Oklahoma), *tsunami, school shooting*, *earthquake*, and *war*. The list could go on and on. One word that we don't think about very often that sends chills down the spine, or at least should, is *plague*. Most people probably don't realize that throughout human history, nothing has killed more people than infectious disease. The death count is astronomical.

In our modern, technologically sophisticated society, we somehow believe that we're impervious to plagues. That they're confined to the pages of history. Even the word *plague* itself conjures up in our minds the ancient picture of Moses and Pharaoh or the medieval bubonic plague that wiped out half of Europe.

For a long time, the general public has not given much thought to a plague. Experts have been sounding the warning for a long time that a super-flu pandemic was coming, but few paid any attention. Somehow plagues seem far-fetched. Until everything changed in early 2020 when COVID-19 erupted in China and swept across the globe. Suddenly, the word *plague*, along with its close cousins *pestilence* and *pandemic*, roared back into the global glossary.

In light of what's happening today, before we look ahead to the end times, I've found it helpful to take a look back at some of the disastrous plagues in the past—plagues mentioned in the Bible and in more recent history. It's always good to look back and look around before we look ahead. As Winston Churchill once said, "The farther backward you can look, the farther forward you are likely to see."[1] With this maxim in mind, let's look back in history as far as we can, so we can see as far ahead in prophecy as we can.

PLAGUES IN THE BIBLE

As we get started, let's define some terms we're all hearing lately. *Merriam-Webster.com Dictionary* defines the English word *pestilence* as "a contagious or infectious epidemic disease that is virulent and devastating" or "something that is destructive or pernicious."[2] Similarly, the definition of the English word *plague* is "an epidemic disease causing a high rate of mortality" or "a disastrous evil or affliction."[3]

The Greek physician Hippocrates was the first person to use the word *epidemic* in a medical sense in 412 BC in reference to an outbreak called the Cough of Perinthus.[4]

The Greek root words for *epidemic* are *epi* ("upon") and *demos* ("people" or "population"), so the term literally means "upon the people."[5]

The term *pandemic*, which came along later, originates from two Greek words and means "all the people," and this word is used today to label a disease that spreads across a vast region of the earth.[6] While coronavirus has not been contracted by all the people, the word *pandemic* is fitting because the virus certainly has spread across the globe and has touched all of us in one way or another.

Turning to the Bible, the word *plague(s)* is found one hundred times in the New King James Version, according to a search at BibleGateway.com. It occurs from Genesis to Revelation. It's found twelve times in the book of Revelation. The word *pestilence(s)* is found forty-four times in the NKJV, with the majority of those instances in the Old Testament prophets of Jeremiah and Ezekiel, who announced God's judgment on Judah and the surrounding nations.

The term *pandemic* is a modern term, so it was never used in the Scriptures. However, ancient Hebrew and Greek words for pestilence and plagues are found at least 127 times in the Bible.[7] Not every use of the words *pestilence* and *plagues* in the Bible refers to a dreadful, infectious disease, but many do.

Of course, we don't have space to list them all. You can look them up in a Bible concordance if you want to read them all, but here are a few notable examples.

In the book of Exodus, God employed dreadful plagues, including ghastly diseases on humans and livestock, to execute judgment against the nation of Egypt and to reveal Himself to the Israelites. Yet it's important to remember that before the judgments began, God directly warned Egypt's leaders of what would occur if they failed to obey God. The Lord graciously warns before He judges.

> Then the LORD said to Moses, "Go to Pharaoh and say to him, 'This is what the LORD, the God of the Hebrews, says: "Let my people go, so that they may worship me." If you refuse to let them go and continue to hold them back, the hand of the LORD will bring a terrible *plague* on your livestock in the field—on your horses, donkeys and camels and on your cattle, sheep and goats.'" (Exodus 9:1–3, emphasis added)

The Philistines experienced a plague that some scholars believe was akin to the bubonic plague when they captured the ark of the covenant from Israel and brought it to their cities.

> So they called together all the rulers of the Philistines and said, "Send the ark of the god of Israel away; let it go back to its own place, or it will kill us and our people." For death had filled the city with panic;

God's hand was very heavy on it. Those who did not die were afflicted with tumors, and the outcry of the city went up to heaven. . . .

The Philistines asked, "What guilt offering should we send to him?"

They replied, "Five gold tumors and five gold rats, according to the number of the Philistine rulers, because the same *plague* has struck both you and your rulers." (1 Samuel 5:11–12; 6:4, emphasis added)

Israel itself was inflicted with a plague as a punishment for King David's sinful numbering of the people. Only when he offered a sacrifice did the Lord relent.

So the Lord sent a *plague* on Israel from that morning until the end of the time designated, and seventy thousand of the people from Dan to Beersheba died. . . .

David built an altar to the Lord there and sacrificed burnt offerings and fellowship offerings. Then the Lord answered his prayer in behalf of the land, and the *plague* on Israel was stopped. (2 Samuel 24:15, 25, emphasis added)

We could go on and on, but one more past example of biblical plagues will suffice. The Hebrew prophet Jeremiah warned of plagues in the days of King Nebuchadnezzar.

> This is what the LORD Almighty, the God of Israel, says: . . . "If, however, any nation or kingdom will not serve Nebuchadnezzar king of Babylon or bow its neck under his yoke, I will punish that nation with the sword, famine and *plague*, declares the LORD, until I destroy it by his hand." (Jeremiah 27:4, 8, emphasis added)

Looking to the future, God will use plagues as part of His destruction of the armies of Gog and Magog, which include the modern nations of Russia and Iran, when they invade the land of Israel in the end times.

> I will summon a sword against Gog on all my mountains, declares the Sovereign LORD. Every man's sword will be against his brother. I will execute judgment on him with *plague* and bloodshed; I will pour down torrents of rain, hailstones and burning sulfur on him and on his troops and on the many nations with him. (Ezekiel 38:21–22, emphasis added)

PLAGUES OF BIBLICAL
PROPORTION

Outside the pages of Scripture, throughout the course of human history, there have been successive waves of plagues, pestilence, disease, illness, and viruses. Many of these waves have been exceedingly deadly. Here's a concise, chilling overview of the worst plagues:

> The plague of Justinian struck in the 6th Century and killed as many as 50 million people, perhaps half the global population at the time. The Black Death of the 14th Century—likely caused by the same pathogen—may have killed up to 200 million people. Smallpox may have killed as many as 300 million people in the 20th Century alone, even though an effective vaccine—the world's first—had been available since 1796.
>
> Some 50 to 100 million people died in the 1918 influenza pandemic—numbers that surpass the death toll of World War One, which was being fought at the same time. The 1918 flu virus infected one in every three people on the planet.... HIV, a pandemic that is still with us and still lacks a vaccine, has killed an estimated 32 million people and infected 75 million, with more added every day.[8]

We often believe that nothing is worse than war, which of course is terrible, but in many ways, pandemics are worse. Axios correspondent Felix Salmon wrote, "Wars are—generally—over when they're over; then the post-war rebuilding can begin. Pandemics don't work that way; their effects reverberate for decades."[9] Below is a chart that shows a timeline of some of the deadliest pandemics on earth.[10]

Pandemics & Time Period	Death Toll
Antonine Plague (165–180)	5 million
Plague of Justinian (541–542)	30–50 million
Japanese Smallpox (735–737)	1 million
Black Death or Bubonic Plague (1347–1351)	200 million
Smallpox (1520)	56 million
Great Plagues (17th–18th centuries)	3.6 million

Cholera 6 Outbreak (1817–1923)	1 million
The Third Plague (1855)	12 million
Yellow Fever (late 1800s)	100–150,000
Russian Flu (1889–90)	1 million
Spanish Flu (1918–19)	40–50 million
Asian Flu (1957–58)	1.1 million
Hong Kong Flu (1968–70)	1 million
HIV/AIDS (1981–present)	25–35 million
SARS (2002–03)	770
Swine Flu (2009–10)	200,000
MERS (2012–present)	850

Ebola (2014–16)	11,300
COVID–19 (2019–20)	67,594 and counting

"Billions of people around the world are living in fear of a lethal and invisible enemy," wrote Salmon. "They're sequestering themselves inside their homes and avoiding human contact . . . because they have internalized the need to do so out of simple self-preservation."[12] As I write, the number of cases and deaths from COVID-19 is rising and has not even peaked in the United States. When we finally get to the other side of this pandemic, I believe the aftershocks of coronavirus could be long-lasting.

SEISMIC SHIFT

We live in a fallen world. Sadly, people die of disease all the time. Clearly, not every disease or outbreak is a sign of the times. In past centuries, as we've seen, the world has suffered devastating death tolls from pandemic plagues. What we see today, in that sense, is no different than what has happened many times in the past. Plagues have been, and continue to be, a tragic part of life on a fallen planet. But what is different today is that the pace is quickening. In the span of forty years, COVID-19 is the sixth infectious plague unleashed on the planet: HIV/AIDS, SARS, swine flu, MERS, Ebola, and now COVID-19.

Coronavirus is a global game-changer that could be a kind of prophetic "shift of gears" with all its eventual fallout. Think about it. There were two deadly flu pandemics in the nineteenth century.[13] There were three in the twentieth century, including the Spanish flu, that's often called "the mother of all pandemics."[14] It was also known as the "Spanish lady" even though it didn't originate in Spain. Up to one in three people fell ill from it, and 5 percent of the global population died, but possibly as high as one in five.[15] Nearly half of the deaths in the United States were young adults twenty to forty years old. The horror and scope of the Spanish flu outbreak is difficult to conceive. John M. Barry described its staggering devastation:

> One cannot know with certainty, but if the upper estimate of the death toll is true as many as 8 to 10 percent of all young adults then living may have been killed by the virus.
>
> And they died with extraordinary ferocity and

speed. Although the influenza pandemic stretched over two years perhaps two-thirds of the deaths occurred in a period of twenty-four weeks, and more than half of those deaths [occurred] in even less time, from mid-September to early December 1918. Influenza killed more people in a year than the Black Plague of the Middle Ages killed in a century; it killed more people in twenty-four weeks than AIDS has killed in twenty-four years.[16]

We've now had our first pandemic plague in the twenty-first century, following several other close calls. Author Bryan Walsh said that COVID-19 is a reminder to us that infectious diseases are very real and should never be overlooked. "In fact, there are more new ones now than ever," he wrote, saying that "the number of new infectious diseases like Sars, HIV and Covid-19 has increased by nearly fourfold over the past century. Since 1980 alone, the number of outbreaks per year has more than tripled."[17] The momentum seems to be building.

In the last decade, it seems like a strange new viral acronym is popping up almost every year. COVID-19 is the most recent plague and the most far-reaching, but we know it won't be the last. This is happening at the same time other storm clouds are gathering on the horizon. Crises on every front are converging and quickening.

From the Scriptures, we see that God warns before He judges. COVID-19 could be an early warning that something bigger is coming. It's a wake-up call for a sleeping world, and we need to open our eyes and look up.

THINGS ARE LOOKING UP

Throughout history, times of global pandemics have always been accompanied by great fear and terror. The same is true today. Fighting an invisible enemy is daunting. People are understandably anxious and frightened. Jesus warned us this would be the case, noting that when the signs of the end of days appear, "People will faint from terror, apprehensive of what is coming on the world" (Luke 21:26). Yet Jesus also told us how to respond in such difficult days. "Now when these things begin to happen, look up and lift up your heads, because your redemption draws near" (Luke 21:28 NKJV).

It's impossible for us to know all the reasons God allows the outbreak of deadly plagues, but one thing is sure. God graciously uses them to wake and shake people, to grab their attention, and to call them to turn their backs on self-sufficiency and trust in Him. Coronavirus is no exception. It's a major wake-up call—maybe a final wake-up call.

Darrell Bock, a New Testament scholar at Dallas Theological Seminary, stated, "Plagues are a way that God seeks to get our attention about our finitude and mortality as well as how we are giving attention to God. They are an opportunity for reflection about how we live and a reminder we are not gods ourselves."[18] Don't miss the opportunity.

In the coming chapters we're going to look around at what's happening today in the headlines and look ahead at end-times Bible prophecy. But let's not forget to heed the words of Jesus and look up.

"Look up, your redemption is drawing near."

The outlook may be dark, but the uplook is always bright.

CHAPTER 4

IS CORONAVIRUS THE JUDGMENT OF GOD?

*I've heard a number of explanations
for the coronavirus. Some suggest it is
like an Old Testament pestilence. . . .
Is it punishment for our collective sins
and forgetting God? I don't know.*

—CAL THOMAS

When disaster strikes, we all have an initial reaction, an immediate response, or a gut feeling. Often it's shock, sympathy, sorrow, or sadness. Or it may be confusion or fear for our own safety. Or we may be moved to prayer for those affected. But one frequent response is secretly wondering if the calamity resulted from sin in the lives of the victims. It happens every time tragedy strikes. Someone always brings up the divine judgment angle, and it's nothing new.

This view of tragedy, especially deadly epidemics, goes all the way back to ancient times, when people frequently believed that divine judgment must be lurking somewhere in the background whenever disaster struck. There's something intuitive within the human heart that knows we're sinful and gravitates toward the notion that natural disasters indicate God is angry with us, particularly when disaster befalls people we consider especially sinful. The ancient Greeks considered disease as spiritual in origin, a punishment from the gods for any kind of misdemeanor.

The 1918 Spanish flu pandemic was widely viewed as an act of God. Many believed it was punishment for World War I, exploitation from colonialism, or people turning away from God.[1] In 1987, 43 percent of Americans viewed AIDS as a divine punishment for sexual immorality.[2] I remember hearing people say that Hurricane Katrina was God's judgment on the "wicked" city of New Orleans.

During the deadly Ebola outbreak in Liberia in 2014–15, Liberia's church leaders claimed it was a plague

God sent to punish the nation. More than one hundred bishops, pastors, general overseers, prophets, evangelists, and other ministers of the gospel who were part of the Liberian Council of Churches passed the following resolution: "God is angry with Liberia, and Ebola is a plague. Liberians have to pray and seek God's forgiveness over the corruption and immoral acts (such as homosexualism, etc.) that continue to penetrate our society. As Christians, we must repent and seek God's forgiveness."[3]

COVID-19 has brought the same response in some circles and the same questions. One evangelical pastor claimed the coronavirus is God's "death angel." He referred to the virus as a "global pandemic" that could kill "hundreds of millions of people." He also said that the virus began in China because of the godless communist government's persecution of Christians and its practice of forced abortions. As for America, he stated,

> God is about to purge a lot of sin off of this planet. Look at the United States, look at the spiritual rebellion in this country—the hatred of God, the hatred of the Bible, the hatred of righteousness. . . . Folks, the Death Angel may be moving right now across the planet. This is the time to get right with God.[4]

An Orthodox Israeli rabbi has claimed that the spread of the deadly coronavirus in Israel and around the world is divine retribution for gay pride parades.[5] On and on we could go.

So, the question remains: Is COVID-19 the judgment of God for the increasing wickedness and rejection of God throughout the world and in the United States?

YES AND NO

The unnuanced answer to the question is yes and no. The longer answer takes a bit more time to tease out. Here are some helpful biblical parameters about plagues.

First, all sickness, disease, and natural disasters are the result of sin. All the misery in the world can be traced back to the original sin of Adam and Eve. Our world is under judgment for sin. Sin caused God's good creation to become a groaning creation.

> The creation was subjected to frustration, not by its own choice, but by the will of the one who subjected it, in hope that the creation itself will be liberated from its bondage to decay and brought into the freedom and glory of the children of God.
>
> We know that the whole creation has been

groaning as in the pains of childbirth right up to the present time. (Romans 8:20–22)

Disease and disasters are groans of a sin-weary world, and the groans are getting deeper and longer. They point to the end of the age. Max Lucado graphically depicted the growing groans this way:

> Nature is a pregnant creation, third-trimester heavy. When a tornado rips through a city in Kansas or an earthquake flattens a region in Pakistan, this is more than barometric changes or shifts of ancient fault lines. The universe is passing through the final hours before delivery. Painful contractions are in the forecast.[6]

The coronavirus points toward these contractions.

Second, some sickness, disease, and natural disasters are the direct result of individual or national sin. The Bible is replete with examples of sickness or plagues falling on individuals, cities, or nations due to sin. These are the targeted judgment of God.

Some judgments, in the form of disease, are past:

- Pharaoh and his house were afflicted with a plague due to Abraham's deception surrounding the true identity of his wife, Sarai (Genesis 12:17).

- Pharaoh and the Egyptians suffered terrible plagues for rejecting God (Exodus 7–12).
- God struck Moses' sister Miriam with leprosy (Numbers 12:1–10).
- The Philistines suffered a terrible disease, which some scholars believe was bubonic plague, for defiling the ark of the covenant (1 Samuel 5:6–12).
- God sent a plague on the people of Israel because of King David's sin (1 Chronicles 21:1–17).

One judgment, in the form of disease, is future:

- The fourth horseman of the Apocalypse will bring pestilence as a judgment of God, wiping out one-fourth of the world's population (Revelation 6:6–8).

Third, no one on earth can say for sure that coronavirus is an outpouring of divine judgment. Why? Because God hasn't said it is. It's that simple. Apart from divine revelation, we can't responsibly say if any modern plague is divine judgment. For anyone to say conclusively that coronavirus is divine judgment is presumptuous and prideful. It's as though the person is saying he or she knows the secret counsels of God that He hasn't chosen to reveal. Here's a good maxim to live by: when God speaks, we must speak; when God is silent, we must be silent. God is silent about the cause of COVID-19, and we must be too.

Those are some simple guidelines to steer us as questions about coronavirus abound.

But is there any further light to shed on how to understand the coronavirus crisis?

WHAT JESUS WOULD SAY TO US ABOUT CORONAVIRUS

On one occasion some people came to Jesus to report a tragic, well-known event that occurred in Jerusalem. "Now there were some present at that time who told Jesus about the Galileans whose blood Pilate had mixed with their sacrifices" (Luke 13:1).

This bloodshed apparently occurred in the temple during Passover, because that was the only time laypeople were allowed to take part in the slaughter of animal sacrifices. So the victims of this tragic event were Galilean pilgrims offering Passover sacrifices in the temple. Evidently, because the Roman governor, Pontius

Pilate, believed these Galileans were guilty of sedition, he had his soldiers attack them when they least expected it. In the melee that ensued, human blood mingled with the river of lambs' blood.[7]

At the root of their report was a theological pre-supposition that the tragedy occurred because the victims were worse sinners than others. The general consensus of the Jewish leaders in Jesus' day was that calamities and misfortunes fell upon those with hidden sins. In other words, good things happen to good people and bad things happen to bad people. We find this attitude in John 9:1–2 and all the way back in the book of Job (4:7–8). As pastor and author Kent Hughes wrote, "This was an attractive way to think about life for those who had been spared adversity. Their goodness, their moral superiority, had spared them! It was all very neat and self-satisfying."[8]

Jesus saw through the thin veneer to the real issue behind the Jewish leaders' report and quickly shut down this viewpoint of tragic events, saying, "Do you think that these Galileans were worse sinners than all the other Galileans because they suffered this way? I tell you, no! But unless you repent, you too will all perish" (Luke 13:2–3). Jesus rejected the common answer to tragedies with a simple negative. Jesus was crystal clear. Those who died were regular old sinners, just like all of us. We all need to repent.

Darrell Bock, a professor at Dallas Theological Seminary, said,

> The issue is not when death will happen or why, but avoiding a terminal fate with even greater consequences. Only repentance will prevent the death that lasts. . . . Without a change of view about Jesus, a black cloud of death hovers over all. This tragedy makes evident the fragile character of life. Jesus issues a call to repent, for disaster looms over the unresponsive.[9]

In His response to the report, Jesus was not denying that sin may bring tragedy. The Bible is clear that sometimes it does bring physical illness (Matthew 9:2; John 5:1–14). But Jesus rejected the idea that all disease or tragedy is due to the sin of its victims.[10]

After initially answering their question, Jesus drove home His point by citing another familiar, tragic incident that transpired in Jerusalem. "Those eighteen who died when the tower in Siloam fell on them—do you think they were more guilty than all the others living in Jerusalem? I tell you, no! But unless you repent, you too will all perish" (Luke 13:4–5).

Jesus said that the message of every plague, tsunami, hurricane, volcanic eruption, and flood is simple: we need to repent. Repent because none of us will escape God's judgment. Since none of us are sinless, we'd better all be prepared.

The word *repent* can sound super spiritual, and many people have a hazy idea of what it really means. In its simplest expression, it means "to change your mind" or "to have another mind." Not what we often think of when we casually change our minds about some decision we've made, but a complete change of mind about Jesus. It's changing from an attitude of unbelief to belief in Jesus as God's Son and our Savior from sin. After the initial act of repentance in turning to Jesus, we must live lives of repentance as we daily seek to turn from our sin.

Philip Henry, an English nonconformist pastor in the seventeenth century, said: "Some people do not like to hear much of repentance. But I think it is necessary, that if I should die in the pulpit, I should desire to die preaching repentance, and if I should die out of the pulpit, I should desire to die practicing it."[11] Martin Luther launched the Reformation by nailing the "Ninety-Five Theses" to the door of Wittenberg Cathedral, and the first thesis stated that "our Lord and Master Jesus Christ . . . willed that the whole life of believers should be repentance."[12]

I believe Jesus' message for us in these turbulent

58

times is: *Change your mind about Me if you've never done so, and then continue to change your daily life to live in conformity with My will.*

FINAL ANSWER

In light of what we've found in Scripture, here are answers to four questions related to COVID-19 and the judgment of God:

1. Is our fallen, sinful world already under judgment? Yes.
2. Can specific diseases or plagues be judgments from God? Yes.
3. Are all diseases or plagues judgments of God? No.
4. Is God warning us of a greater future judgment to come and calling us to be ready? Yes.

Yes, all disease and disaster are ultimately the result of the fall of man and original sin. We live and move in a fallen world that's not what it was intended to be. But I don't believe the coronavirus is the result of a specific sin of any individual or nation, based on the information we have available to us. However, like all other disasters, it's a sobering reminder to examine and evaluate our lives. It's an urgent call to consider where we stand with God and to take stock of our lives as the end draws near.

Pastor and author Timothy Keller said,

> When people die in a disaster that does not mean God is judging them. What He's actually trying to do is show that they're no worse than anybody else. . . . But what God is trying to do is trying to get our attention. It's just a way, I do think, for God to try to wake us up and to say, please make sure you're right with me. Please think, think about, you know, where you are.[13]

The question we should be asking, in light of coronavirus, is not *Is this the judgment of God?* The pertinent question is *Am I right with God?* This means the current crisis affords each of us a unique opportunity. The coronavirus contagion is a wake-up call, a piercing alarm, urging everyone to turn to Jesus and then come clean every day by turning away from anything in our lives that is not pleasing to God. It's an opportunity to make sure we're ready for the any-moment coming of Christ, which all signs indicate could be very soon.

Here's the outlook we should adopt:

Every outbreak of pestilence, whether a localized epidemic or a global pandemic, should remind us of the Lord's words, and force the question upon us, "Am I ready for Christ's return? Have I bowed the knee to Jesus as Lord? Am I living the faithful, godly life he has called me to? Will I be put to shame at his appearing?" The coronavirus should impress upon us afresh that this world is passing away, that history is not going round in circles but heading towards a great and terrible Day of judgment.[14]

As disconcerting, disheartening, and daunting as coronavirus is, you and I need to view it as a providential opportunity to get our priorities and perspective in line with God's will as we await the coming of Christ. From a health standpoint, COVID-19 is real and serious and should not be underestimated or minimized. But from a spiritual perspective, coronavirus affords us all a unique season to prepare for what lies ahead—to get ready to meet the Lord.

Make the most of the opportunity. Seize it. Don't let it go to waste.

CHAPTER 5

PESTILENCE IN VARIOUS PLACES

In the last days perilous times will come.
—APOSTLE PAUL, 2 TIMOTHY 3:1 NKJV

O n Wednesday, April 1, AD 33, Jesus preached His
final great sermon. It was a kind of farewell address.
Within the brief span of forty-eight hours, He would be
betrayed, arrested, tried, convicted, beaten, mocked, and
finally nailed to a Roman torture rack known as a cross.
However, at this point, the cross was still two days away.
Jesus' closest followers still had no idea what was coming,
but crucifixion was the furthest thing from their minds.

After a long, tense day of confrontation in the temple precincts with the religious leaders, Jesus and His beleaguered band of twelve made their way out of the temple area for the final time during Jesus' ministry. As they left, the disciples paused and pointed to the stunningly beautiful buildings on the temple mount. Then Jesus dropped a bombshell when He asked them, "Do you see all these things? . . . Truly I tell you, not one stone here will be left on another; every one will be thrown down" (Matthew 24:2).

Think about hearing someone predict the destruction of one of the iconic buildings of the modern world: the White House, the Empire State Building, Buckingham Palace, the Sydney Opera House, the Sistine Chapel, or the Louvre. You'd be shocked. You would want some details, wouldn't you? Jesus' disciples certainly did.[1]

After they had crossed the deep ravine known as the Kidron Valley and ascended the western slope of the Mount of Olives, Jesus reached a stopping point and sat down on one of the many rocks that littered the hillside. Desperately in search of more details about Jesus' forecast, the four closest disciples (Peter, James, John, and Andrew) approached Him privately and asked, "When will this happen, and what will be the sign of your coming and of the end of the age?" (v. 3). The disciples asked three questions, but in their minds, it was really one big question, because to them the destruction of Jerusalem and the temple would signify the end of the age (Zechariah 12–14). These were inseparably connected in their thinking. Seen in this light, the question they really wanted answered was: "When will the end come?" followed by the related question "How will we know when it's near?"

Sitting there in full view of the temple two hundred feet below, as the sun lowered and the shadows lengthened over the city, Jesus, the preeminent prophet, issued an urgent "Danger Ahead" kind of warning. Pivoting off their question about the coming destruction of the temple, which would happen about forty years later in AD 70, Jesus opened a window into the more distant future in the end times.

> Jesus answered: "Watch out that no one deceives you. For many will come in my name, claiming, 'I am the Messiah,' and will deceive many. You will hear of wars and rumors of wars, but see to it that you are not alarmed. Such things must happen, but the end is still to come. Nation will rise against nation, and kingdom against kingdom. There will be famines and earthquakes in various places. All these are the beginning of birth pains." (Matthew 24:4–8)

Luke's gospel provides a parallel account of Jesus' sermon, adding pestilence or plagues to the list of terminal signs.

> He replied: "Watch out that you are not deceived. For many will come in my name, claiming, 'I am he,' and, 'The time is near.' Do not follow them. When you hear of wars and uprisings, do not be frightened. These things must happen first, but the end will not come right away." Then he said to them: "Nation will rise against nation, and kingdom against kingdom. There will be great earthquakes, famines and pestilences in various places, and fearful events and great signs from heaven." (Luke 21:8–11)

There is no place in the Bible that gives a clearer, more concise overview of what's going to happen during earth's final days than the basic outline of the last days Jesus gave in His Olivet Discourse. For that reason, it's often called the mini-apocalypse.

THE BEGINNING OF THE END

Jesus said many things in this great discourse, but one big idea cannot be overlooked or dismissed: this world is not going to become a better place to live. Things are going to get bad—really bad!—before they get better. Those who believe the world is going to get better and better are in for a rude awakening. Jesus held no such false hope for the world. To the contrary, Jesus gave His disciples and us a foreboding forecast, a dark description of what we should look for as the end draws near. The world is not "ascending to utopia but descending to pandemonium."[2]

Times of almost unbelievable, unique calamity are on the horizon. Nothing in all of world history will compare to what is coming in the end of days. It will totally eclipse all that's come before. As Philip De Courcy said, "During the last days of human history, the atmosphere will be thick with a foreboding sense of the climactic and catastrophic."[3] Jesus said it plainly: "For then there will be great distress, unequaled from the beginning of the world until now—and never to be equaled again" (Matthew 24:21). Jesus didn't pull any punches. No one can accuse Him of sugarcoating what lies ahead.

In Matthew 24, Jesus began His forecast with end-time *prophecies* (vv. 4–31) and then moved to end-time *parables* (vv. 32–46). Anticipating what lies ahead and then applying it to the hearts and lives of His listeners, He began His powerful, prophetic forecast by listing three main signposts that will mark the road to the beginning of the end. Jesus laid out three signature events that will indicate history is bumping up against the end of the age.[4]

1. Heresy: "Watch out that no one deceives you. For many will come in my name, claiming, 'I am the Messiah,' and will deceive many" (v. 4).
2. Rivalry: "You will hear of wars and rumors of wars, but see to it that you are not alarmed. Such things must happen, but the end is still to come. Nation will rise against nation, and kingdom against kingdom" (vv. 6–7).
3. Calamity: "There will be famines, pestilences, and earthquakes in various places" (v. 7 NKJV).

Deception, wars, and natural disasters will increase exponentially in the end of days, telegraphing the return of Christ. Jesus called these the "beginning of birth pains" (v. 8). In other words, these are the initial signs that the end is near, the beginning of the end. Like birth pains, the calamities of the end times will strengthen in intensity and get closer together as the end draws near. They will increase dramatically in intensity and frequency.

CORONA CONTRACTIONS

There are several views of the timing of the events in Matthew 24.[5] Many believe the birth-pain signs in verses 4–14 are unfolding in the present. When natural disasters or diseases erupt, it's common for Christian pastors and teachers to see them as signs of doomsday. Earthquakes, hurricanes, and floods are often directly related to end-times prophecies. Back in 2014 when Ebola was ravaging the west coast of Africa, many saw it as a possible fulfillment of Jesus' prediction of pestilence in the end times.[6]

In the same way, many people today believe the outbreak of the coronavirus is one of these beginning contractions Jesus predicted. For example, one Bible prophecy teacher, who I like very much and is a friend of mine, said, "I believe what we are witnessing with COVID-19 is part of the birth pains Jesus talked about in the Olivet Discourse. In fact, I think it is a major birth pain, as is the locust plague that is ravaging Africa and the Mideast; as is the large number of social uprisings in countries around the world; as is the increase in earthquake activity; as were the record-breaking Australian wild fires; as is . . . you get the picture. Birth pains increase in frequency and intensity and continue to do so until the moment of delivery."[7] I understand his sentiment, and it's one that's held by many solid prophecy teachers.

Anne Graham Lotz suggested COVID-19 could be one of the birth pains Jesus predicted. "As I reflect on all the above, I remember the words of Jesus. He warned us that at the end of time there would be pestilences. In the last few years, we have endured SARS, the swine flu, Ebola, avian flu, MERS, West Nile virus, and now the coronavirus. Could COVID-19 be one more sign that our redemption is drawing near? Is the End in sight? Is Jesus coming . . . soon?"[8] Many other well-known Christians leaders could be cited who agree with this view.

My position is that I believe coronavirus is prophetically significant, but I don't believe it's one of the birth pains Jesus predicted in His final sermon. I believe the birth pains will be fulfilled in the final days of tribulation that immediately precede the return of Jesus. Let me give you four points to support my view.

First, viewing the birth pains as general signs during this present age fails to do justice to their severity. How can they serve as signs if they've been occurring for hundreds of years?

There have always been false Christs, wars, earthquakes, famines, and plagues. Those who place the birth pains in the present point out that they are intensifying, but how intense do they have to become to serve as signs? When wars, famines, earthquakes, and plagues slam the earth during the tribulation, there will be no doubt they have arrived. The signs will be clear to all.

Second, a pregnant woman does not experience labor pains until very near or shortly before delivery time. In the same way, the events connected with the Lord's return will not begin until just before His return and will be compressed into a short period of time. After they begin, they will accelerate, escalating to an explosion of catastrophic events.[9]

Third, the apostle Paul employed the image of birth pains in referring to the judgment of the end times. "Now, brothers and sisters, about times and dates we do not need to write to you, or you know very well that the day of the Lord will come like a thief in the night. While people are saying, 'Peace and safety,' destruction will come on them suddenly, as labor pains on a pregnant woman, and they will not escape" (1 Thessalonians 5:1–3). Paul placed the birth pains in the future day of the Lord, which is another term for the tribulation. This supports the future view of the plagues in Luke 21:11.

Fourth, there are striking parallels between Matthew 24 (and Luke 21) and Revelation 6–7, as seen on the next page.

Jesus' Olivet Discourse	Revelation 6–7
False christs (Matt. 24:4–5)	Rider on the white horse (6:1–2)
Wars and rumors of wars (Matt. 24:6–7)	Rider on the red horse (6:3–4)
Famines and earthquakes (Matt. 24:7)	Rider on the black horse (6:5–6)
Famines and plagues (Matt. 24:7; Luke 21:11)	Rider on the pale horse (6:7–8)
Persecution and martyrdom (Matt. 24:9–10)	Martyrs (6:9–11)
Terrors and great cosmic signs (Luke 21:11)	Terror (6:12–17)

| Worldwide preaching of the gospel (Matt. 24:14) | Ministry of the 144,000 (7:1–8) |

The seal judgments in Revelation 6 clearly correspond to the future tribulation period when the rider on the white horse, the coming Antichrist, will be on the march. The close linkage between Jesus' predictions and Revelation 6 necessitates placing them in the same setting.

For these reasons, I put the plagues Jesus mentioned in Luke 21 during the first half of the coming tribulation that will come after the rapture. They are the beginning of birth pains that will ultimately lead to the delivery of God's kingdom on earth.

Many excellent, respected commentators agree that the plagues of Luke 21:11 and the other birth pains are still future, even today. Warren Wiersbe said,

Matthew 24:1–44 indicates that our Lord was discussing events that will take place on earth during the time of Tribulation. . . . After the church has been suddenly taken out of the world, there will be a period of "peace and safety" (1 Thess. 5:1–4) followed by a time of terrible suffering. Many Bible scholars believe this period will last seven years (Dan. 9:24–27). It is this period of "Tribulation" that Jesus described in the Olivet Discourse. At the end of that period, Jesus will return to the earth, defeat His foes, and establish the promised kingdom.[10]

Wiersbe later added: "Jesus said that wars, earthquakes, pestilence, and famines by themselves are not signs of His soon return. These things have been going on throughout the history of the world. However, during the first half of the Tribulation, these events will multiply and intensify."[11]

John MacArthur also believes that Jesus' Olivet Discourse points to the future:

It seems more sensible and more consistent, therefore, to take a futurist approach with respect to the Olivet Discourse. . . . These are events that will immediately precede Christ's coming to establish His kingdom, and therefore they are events that are yet future even today. That seems to be the sense conveyed by the passage itself (e.g., vv. 29–31), and it is the interpretation I believe the text demands.[12]

So, this raises an important question: Does the coronavirus have any relevance to the end times? I believe it does. I believe the coronavirus is a faint, yet frightening, foreshadow or preview of what's coming.

PLAGUES AND PREMATURE
LABOR PAINS

Think of how the COVID-19 pandemic changed the world in such a short time. Multiply those weeks and months many times, and you'll have a faint glimpse of how the birth-pain plagues will jar the world during the tribulation. The coronavirus is a small window into what is to come. Speaking of the effect of these future events, Jesus said, "People will faint from terror, apprehensive of what is coming on the world" (Luke 21:26). The rapid spread of coronavirus and the ensuing panic show how ripe the world is for the contractions of deadly pestilence that will sweep the globe. John MacArthur seems to agree with that assumption:

> That doesn't mean the era we are living in is the one Christ describes. But it *does* underscore the imminency of Christ's return for the church. The world in which we live is already ripe for the Tribulation. Elements like the birth-pang signs are already being felt. The present afflictions may merely be like Braxton-Hicks contractions—premature labor pains—but they nonetheless signify that the time for hard labor, and then delivery, is inevitable and quickly drawing near.[13]

That's a great analogy. Recent events, including the coronavirus, are not the birth pains Jesus forecasted, but they signify premature labor pains—Braxton Hicks contractions, if you will—pointing to a time that is coming . . . and may be coming very soon.

IT'S NOT THE END

In His great end-times sermon, Jesus fortified His followers with farsighted courage. He adjusted their perspective. He listed the calamities of life but then pointed His disciples to the end. He encouraged and energized them with the truth of His coming. The birth pains are coming for sure. Make no mistake. But when those birth pains are over, the delivery will come as Jesus returns and brings heaven to earth. "At that time they will see the Son of Man coming in a cloud with power and great glory. When these things begin to take place, stand up and lift up your heads, because your redemption is drawing near" (Luke 21:27–28).

There's something about knowing things will all work out in the end that strengthens us to stand strong and endure even in the midst of trying, turbulent times. Knowing and trusting in final triumph creates firm tenacity. In his book *Fearless*, Max Lucado wrote about Admiral James Stockdale, who was held as a prisoner of war for eight years during the Vietnam War. After his release, Admiral Stockdale was asked how in the world he survived eight years in a prisoner-of-war camp.

He replied, "I never lost faith in the end of the story. I never doubted not only that I would get out, but also that I would prevail in the end and turn the experience into the defining event of my life, which, in retrospect, I would not trade."

When asked who did not make it out, Admiral Stockdale replied, "Oh, that's easy. The optimists. . . . they were the ones who said, 'We're going to be out by Christmas.' And Christmas would come, and Christmas would go. Then they'd say, 'We're going to be out by Easter.' And Easter would come, and Easter would go. And then Thanksgiving, and then it would be Christmas again. And they died of a broken heart."

Lucado concluded this story by saying, "Real courage embraces the twin realities of current difficulty and ultimate triumph. Yes, life stinks. But it won't forever. As one of my friends likes to say, 'Everything will work out in the end. If it's not working out, it's not the end.'"[14]

I'm sure we would all agree that many things are not working out as we'd like, especially in recent days, which tells us it's not the end. That's the hope with which we need to live. Jesus is coming. Everything will work out in the end.

The world is shaking, and Jesus wants us to know that things are not going to get better in the short term. But for believers in Jesus Christ, the best is yet to come. We have a kingdom that cannot be shaken (Hebrews 12:28). You can read about that kingdom and the end of your story in Revelation 21–22. Here's a brief sample.

> Then I saw "a new heaven and a new earth," for the first heaven and the first earth had passed away, and there was no longer any sea. I saw the Holy City, the new Jerusalem, coming down out of heaven from God, prepared as a bride beautifully dressed for her husband. And I heard a loud voice from the throne saying, "Look! God's dwelling place is now among the people, and he will dwell with them. They will be his people, and God himself will be with them and be their God. 'He will wipe every tear from their eyes. There will be no more death or mourning or crying or pain, for the old order of things has passed away.'"
>
> He who was seated on the throne said, "I am making everything new!" Then he said, "Write this down, for these words are trustworthy and true."

He said to me: "It is done. I am the Alpha and the Omega, the Beginning and the End. To the thirsty I will give water without cost from the spring of the water of life. Those who are victorious will inherit all this, and I will be their God and they will be my children." (21:1–7)

Don't lose faith in the end of the story. No matter what happens.

Our ultimate triumph in Jesus Christ is sure.

CHAPTER 6

THUNDERING HOOFBEATS OF THE PALE RIDER

*Of the Four Horsemen of the
Apocalypse, the one named War
has gone—at least for a while. But
Famine, Pestilence and Death are
still charging over the earth.*

—US President Herbert Hoover

think it's safe to say that one of the best-known prophecies in the Bible, and in the book of Revelation, is the four horsemen of the Apocalypse. The vivid imagery found in Revelation 6:1–8 has captivated readers for two thousand years.

> Then I saw when the Lamb broke one of the seven seals, and I heard one of the four living creatures saying as with a voice of thunder, "Come." I looked, and behold, a white horse, and he who sat on it had a bow; and a crown was given to him, and he went out conquering and to conquer.
>
> When He broke the second seal, I heard the second living creature saying, "Come." And another, a red horse, went out; and to him who sat on it, it was granted to take peace from the earth, and that men would slay one another; and a great sword was given to him.
>
> When He broke the third seal, I heard the third living creature saying, "Come." I looked, and behold, a black horse; and he who sat on it had a pair of scales in his hand. And I heard something like a voice in the center of the four living creatures saying, "A quart of wheat for a denarius, and three quarts of barley for a denarius; and do not damage the oil and the wine."
>
> When the Lamb broke the fourth seal, I heard the voice of the fourth living creature saying, "Come." I

looked, and behold, an ashen horse; and he who sat on it had the name Death; and Hades was following with him. Authority was given to them over a fourth of the earth, to kill with sword and with famine and with pestilence and by the wild beasts of the earth. (NASB)

Billy Graham authored a powerful, riveting book titled *Approaching Hoofbeats: The Four Horsemen of the Apocalypse*. In that book, he penned these words:

Some theologians and Bible scholars have thought these scenes as described by the Apostle John to be a description of past events. However, most evangelical scholars interpret them as having to do with the future—as do I. In my view, the shadows of all four horsemen can already be seen galloping throughout the world at this moment; therefore, I not only want to apply these four symbols of events yet to come, but also to put our ears to the ground and hear their hoofbeats growing louder by the day. . . .

I can hear the hoofbeats of these horses much louder than when I first began writing this book.[1]

Almost forty years have passed since that book's release, and if the sound of the four horsemen's hoofbeats could be heard approaching then, how much closer are they today? In the 2020s, those *approaching* hoofbeats have now become *thundering* hoofbeats. We can put our ear to the ground and hear them approaching and possibly feel the earth shaking beneath them.

RIDERS ON THE STORM

Revelation 6 introduced a dramatic change from Revelation 4–5 as Scriptures shift from heaven to earth, from divine worship to divine wrath. No longer do we see a throne in heaven, angels flying around the throne, twenty-four elders casting their crowns before God's feet, or heavenly choirs singing praises. The worshiping creatures around the throne are replaced by the wrath of the four horsemen.

Talk about coming back to earth!

The four horsemen of the Apocalypse are the first four seals on a seven-sealed scroll that is opened by Jesus. The scroll represents a will that transfers the full inheritance of the nations to Jesus from His Father. Jesus receives the inheritance when the scroll is opened and He returns to earth.

The four horses, or what we might call "the final four," were white, red, black, and pale (ashen). The imagery of different colored horses hearkened back to the Old Testament prophet Zechariah (1:7–17; 6:1–8). We want to focus our attention on the fourth horse in Revelation 6—the pale rider—but to get the complete context, let's look at all four horses and their riders, since they fit together as a unit.

Each of the first four seals followed the same pattern:

1. Christ broke the seal.
2. One of the four living creatures called out, "Come."
3. A different colored horse with a rider galloped across the landscape.

The four horses and their riders depicted the initial events that will occur at the beginning of the final time of global tribulation after the rapture of all believers to heaven. The complete tribulation period is described in detail in Revelation 6–18.

The evil quartet of the four horsemen corresponded to what Jesus prophesied about the end times in His sermon on the Mount of Olives two days before He died. Jesus referred to these judgments as "the beginning of birth pains" (Matthew 24:8) or, as the King James Version says, "the beginning of sorrows." Max Lucado noted, "Painful contractions are in the forecast."[2]

COUNTERFEIT CHRIST

The rider on the white horse in Revelation 6:2 is not Christ. He is the Antichrist. He is a counterfeit, mimic, or parody of the true Christ who rides a white horse in Revelation 19. He is the dark prince who claims to be the light. The contrast between the rider of Revelation 6 and the rider of Revelation 19 is striking:

> The Antichrist has a bow but no arrows. Christ wields a mighty sword.
>
> Antichrist wears a victor's crown. Christ wears many crowns.
>
> Antichrist initiates wars. Christ returns to earth to end all wars.
>
> Antichrist commences the great tribulation. Christ closes the great tribulation.

The rider on the white horse has a bow but no arrows, which indicates that his initial conquest and takeover, at the beginning of the tribulation, is diplomatic and bloodless. He will rise to power on a platform of peace in the midst of unprecedented global upheaval and turmoil in the wake of the rapture. He will be hailed as the greatest diplomat and peacemaker the world has ever known. He will sign a peace treaty with

Israel, solving the stubborn, decades-old Middle East crisis (Daniel 9:27). In a broader stroke, he will introduce a brief interval of world peace (1 Thessalonians 5:1–3). He'll undoubtedly win the Nobel Peace Prize and be *Time* magazine's Man of the Year. In a world with growing complexity and chaos, he will be the man the world has been waiting for.

Our world today is increasingly ripe for his arrival.

SEEING RED

The red horse of Revelation 6:4 is described in the original Greek language as *pyrros* or "fiery red." The horse and its rider symbolize the wars that will erupt in the end times. This horse parallels Jesus' prophecy in Matthew 24:6–7, which talked about "wars and rumors of wars" and how "nation will rise against nation, and kingdom against kingdom."

The red color symbolizes the awful horror of slaughter and bloodshed that will accompany these wars. The image of warfare is reinforced by the large sword in the rider's hand and the statement that he will take peace from the earth. The red horse will disrupt the peace the rider on the white horse was able to temporarily forge.

HUNGER GAMES

Often following a war there are more deaths from famine, disease, and epidemics than there were from actual battles. That will be the case in the end times. The war horse is followed by the tar-black horse with a rider holding in his hand a pair of scales on which he is carefully weighing food. The black horse of Revelation 6:5–6 represents a famine so severe that it will take a denarius—an entire day's wages to the original readers of this text—to buy a measure of wheat or three measures of barley. In other words, the world will experience runaway hyperinflation. Food prices will be so high that it will cost a day's earnings just to buy enough food for one meal for an average person.

As John Walvoord wrote: "To put it in ordinary language, the situation would be such that one would have to spend a day's wages for a loaf of bread with no money left to buy anything else. The symbolism therefore indicates a time of famine when life will be reduced to the barest necessities."[3]

PALE RIDER

With each successive horseman, the severity of the judgment intensifies. The pale horse is no exception, and the rider on this haunting horse in Revelation 6:7–8 wreaks untold destruction. The horse's color is ashen or pale. The Greek word is *chloros*, from which we get the English words *chlorine* or *chlorophyll*. *Chloros* normally denotes a pale green color and is used twice in Revelation to describe the color of grass and vegetation (8:7; 9:4). In Revelation 6:8, however, it pictures the color of a decomposing corpse. New Testament professor Robert Thomas described the putrid color of the fourth horse as "the yellowish green of decay, the pallor of death. It is the pale ashen color that images a face bleached because of terror. It recalls a corpse in the advanced state of corruption."[4]

The fourth horse and rider possess two features that set them apart from the first three. First, the name of the rider is stated. There's no doubt about his identity. His name is *Death*. The rider on this horse is the grim reaper.

The second distinctive feature of the pale rider is his macabre associate. Wherever Death rides, he is trailed by Hades. In the Greek New Testament, the word *Hades* occurs ten times. It refers to the compartment of the underworld or netherworld where the souls of lost people are imprisoned while awaiting the final judgment day. At that time, the souls in Hades will come forth, and after the final verdict is rendered, they will be thrown into *Gehenna*, or the lake of the fire, as their final, everlasting abode.

Hades is personified. He shadows the pale rider. The two are inseparable. The text doesn't state whether Hades is also mounted or is on foot, but either way, as Death stalks his prey, Hades follows right behind to gulp down the carnage littered in his dreadful aftermath. Hades acts as Death's hearse. Charles Swindoll graphically described the pale rider and his shadow in this way:

> In this terrifying scene, John saw the grim reaper and the grave digger moving together across the face of the earth. Death slays the body while Hades swallows up the soul. These two symbols represent the massive number of deaths that will follow in the wake of the first three horsemen. One-quarter of the world's population will be lost in their rampage.[5]

Near the end of the movie *Tombstone*, Wyatt Earp pointed a shotgun at Ike Clanton and said, "You tell 'em I'm coming! And Hell's coming with me, you hear! Hell's coming with me!" The pale rider could say the same thing. "Hell's coming with me."

The rider Death will inflict unspeakable carnage, and the planet will be strewn with the remains of his victims. The magnitude of the mayhem is difficult to wrap your mind around. Allow these somber words to sink in: "Authority was given to them over a fourth of the earth, to kill with sword and with famine and with pestilence and by the wild beasts of the earth" (Revelation 6:8 NASB).

One-fourth of the earth!

Twenty-five percent of the world's population will perish at the hands of the pale rider within a very brief span of time. That's well over 1.5 billion people with today's population. They'll be swept away by Death and then gobbled up by his henchman Hades. Billy Graham described the effect of the pale rider: "Death casts its shadow over the land. On every continent, in every nation, and through every city, town, and village death rides unfettered. It brings hardship, suffering and sorrow wherever it goes."[6]

And as mind-numbing as this judgment is, we have to recall that Jesus referred to this event as "merely the beginning of birth pangs" of the final days of tribulation (Matthew 24:7–8 NASB). The worst will be yet to come.

WHY?

Reading texts like this often causes people to wonder about the goodness of God. We ask the "why" question. Why will God do this? How can a kind, loving God unleash this kind of carnage? How can God be good and at the same time be connected to such destruction?

When questions like these are raised, believers often respond by saying that God doesn't *cause* catastrophes; He simply *allows* them to happen. That's certainly true in some cases, but the four horsemen of the Apocalypse are unleashed by Jesus, the Lamb. He's responsible for them. He opened each of the seals, sending forth judgment. There's no way for us to skirt His direct involvement in these catastrophes. So how can we explain this?

I don't profess to understand the depth of God's wisdom and ways, but Scripture is clear that God is infinitely just and holy and that He must judge sin and wickedness. A deity who overlooks evil is no deity at all. God's righteousness demands a day of reckoning for sin. To be sure, God is infinitely gracious, loving, and merciful. But after millennia of patience and mercy, God's long-suffering will finally reach its end in the final day of the Lord. Judgment is just as much a part of God's nature and character as love and mercy. As John MacArthur stated:

> But while the Bible is a book of hope, it is also a book of judgment. Because God loves righteousness and faith, He must hate sin and unbelief. He cannot love

truth unless He hates lies. He cannot love goodness unless He hates wickedness. He cannot reward
unless He also punishes.[7]

One hint of God's purpose in these judgments is that
Jesus called them "birth pains," which indicates they're
more than just retribution. They're an integral part of a
necessary process that will result in the delivery of new
life and a new world for God's people. God has a glorious
purpose to establish His rule on earth through His Son,
but before the new world can be inaugurated, God must
judge those who have despised and defiled His holiness
and refused to accept His gracious offer of salvation. The
pale rider will be one wave of the intense contractions
that will ultimately bring about the delivery of God's
kingdom on earth in which righteousness dwells.

FOUR OF A KIND

The pale rider will employ four means to inflict his
misery on the earth and its inhabitants, as described in
Revelation 6:8.

Sword—The first means by which the final rider
slays his victims is the sword. This reminds us

of the second seal, the red rider, and speaks of warfare that will persist and continue to rack up its body count as the tribulation rushes on. Millions will die as the earth is overrun with bloody wars.

Famine—The pale rider's second weapon is famine. This calls to mind the third seal, the dark rider. The famine launched by the black horse will intensify as its dark shroud envelops the earth.

Pestilence—War and famine will continue to plague the earth, breaking out in various places, but now a new horror is added: *pestilence*. In the original Greek, the word is *thanato*, which generally means "death." In this instance, however, it refers to death by means of pestilence, plague, or disease. Sword, famine, and pestilence are frequently linked together in the Old Testament (1 Chronicles 21:12; Jeremiah 14:12; 21:7; 24:10; 44:13; Ezekiel 5:12; 6:11–12).

Moreover, as we saw in chapter 4, Jesus' blueprint of end-time signs in Luke 21:11 listed "pestilences," or plagues, as one of the final judgments. And Revelation 6:8 mentions the same four judgments, echoing Ezekiel, who called them God's four severe judgments: "For thus says the Lord GOD, 'How much more when I send My four severe judgments against Jerusalem: sword, famine, wild beasts and plague to cut off man and beast from it!'" (Ezekiel 14:21 NASB).

Wild Beasts of the Earth—The fourth destructive force of the pale rider is "the wild beasts of the earth." Not surprisingly, this reference has generated some diverse views. There are three main interpretations of these wild beasts.

First, this could refer to literal wild animals that will become unrestrained and ferocious during the tribulation. In the chaos of the end times, they would search for prey, taking advantage of the weak and defenseless.[8] Support for this idea is found in several Old Testament verses.

> I will send wild animals against you, and they will rob you of your children, destroy your cattle and make you so few in number that your roads will be deserted. (Leviticus 26:22)

> I will send wasting famine against them,
>   consuming pestilence and deadly plague;
> I will send against them the fangs of wild beasts,
>   the venom of vipers that glide in the dust.
>   (Deuteronomy 32:24)

> "I will send four kinds of destroyers against
> them," declares the LORD, "the sword to kill and the
> dogs to drag away and the birds and the wild animals
> to devour and destroy." (Jeremiah 15:3)

While this view is certainly possible, the problem
I have is that it seems implausible that crazed animals
could have such a devastating impact as set forth in
Revelation 6:8.

Second is the view that "the wild beasts of the earth"
is a reference to military and political leaders who mur-
der and slaughter people all over the earth during the
end times.[9] This view is based on the usage in Revelation
of the term *wild beast* (*theerion* in Greek). The word is
found thirty-eight times in Revelation, and in every
instance it refers to the Beast (the Antichrist) and his lieu-
tenant, the false prophet. These two men are described
in detail in Revelation 13. The term *wild beasts* is a vivid
way to describe the vicious character of brutal dictators
who have no regard for human life.

While either one of the first two views is certainly
possible, many excellent commentators and Bible
teachers believe in a third view, which refers to "wild
beasts of the earth" as diseases and pandemic plagues
that are transmitted from animals to humans.[10] I
agree with this view because of the close connection

between "pestilence" and the "wild beasts of the earth" in Revelation 6:8. At this point, Revelation 6 intersects deeply with what we see today with coronavirus and other plagues that have fallen upon us. The late Adrian Rogers wrote this:

> What kind of animal do you think of when you think of a beast? A bear? A tiger? A rhinoceros? Beasts come in many sizes. If you look up the word in a dictionary, the definition may define a beast only as a four-footed mammal.
>
> Do you know what beasts carried the Black Death? Rats. These tiny four-footed mammals carried a bubonic bacterium that killed more than twenty-five million people in a five-year period.[11]

The devastating effect of rats is well known in history, but today the denotation of wild beasts of the earth has expanded to include bats, mosquitos, monkeys, pigs, and birds. Deadly viruses are hopping from animals to humans at an alarming rate. A disease moving from animals to humans is often called a "spillover." Our world is ripe for the global spillover of the pale rider. The stage could not be more perfectly set for the fourth horseman to begin his ride. The plagues from wild beasts of the earth are multiplying and intensifying.

Animal-borne plagues that jump or cross over from animals to humans are called zoonotic diseases. A host of them have appeared throughout history, but they've mushroomed in the last few decades. Here are a few examples of zoonotic diseases:

- Bubonic plague—carried by rodents and even cats; passed to humans through bites from infected fleas (often rat fleas)
- Rabies—transmitted through a bite from an infected animal, usually dogs or bats
- Malaria—transmitted by mosquitos
- Dengue fever—transmitted by mosquitos
- Spanish flu—killed 50 million people worldwide; source was avian (birds), an H1N1 virus
- AIDS/HIV—traced to a type of chimpanzee in Central Africa
- Lyme disease—comes from infected ticks
- Ebola—first identified in 1976; comes from infected bats
- SARS—identified in 2003, originating in bats
- MERS—identified in 2012, originating in bats and passed to camels
- Avian (bird) flu—transmitted by birds
- Swine flu—outbreak began in 2009; comes from pigs

According to the Centers for Disease Control and Prevention (CDC), three out of every four new or emerging infectious diseases in people come from animals.[12] That's staggering. Seventy-five percent of all new diseases cross from animals to humans. Al Mohler noted the role animals play in so many plagues:

> Now we're talking about a coronavirus, and one of the interesting and troubling things about this kind of virus is that it appears to emerge primarily from animals, transmitted from animal to animal until some kind of mutation allows the transmission from animal to human, but the most frightening mutation takes place when the virus mutates in order to spread from human to human. . . . Now, one of the reasons so many of these viruses start out in places like China is because there is a closer proximity between human beings and animals. Not only that, but animals and other animals. We are told that some of these viruses, these coronaviruses, exist naturally within bat populations, the bat populations then spread it to other populations. Often you hear about the role [played] by swine, by pigs in this process, because pigs are often the engine or the context for the mutation of the virus into a new form.[13]

An article in *Newsweek* further highlighted the dramatic rise of animal diseases jumping to humans:

> This novel coronavirus is a classic example of the emergence of new microbial threats and their spread. The vast majority of the new infectious diseases that have presented in recent decades have come from animals. . . . But simply said, these so-called zoonotic pathogens live in animals or are carried by insects and then "jump" to humans. When they jump, they can cause new diseases that we haven't had to deal with before, like 2019-nCoV. Unfortunately, we're seeing the emergence of several new zoonotic diseases each year—any of which may become the next pandemic.[14]

New diseases are emerging at an alarming rate. Some are more deadly than others, but "on average, in one corner of the world or another, a new infectious disease has emerged every year for the past 30 years."[15] That's at least thirty new diseases that have cropped up in just the last thirty years. COVID-19 is the newest one. In her book *Pale Rider: The Spanish Flu of 1918 and How It Changed the World*, Laura Spinney included a chapter that's chillingly titled "Beware the Barnyard," in which she warned of emerging diseases that are spilling over from animals to humans.[16]

These new diseases are erupting at the same time globalism and rapid means of travel are expanding to provide the perfect vehicle to spread these plagues all over the earth with lightning speed. Coronavirus may just be the first of a new wave of pestilence that explodes across our planet. The pale horse is ready to sweep the globe, with Hades racing right behind.

The pandemic plagues of the end times will have repercussions beyond the plagues themselves. These plagues will further the argument of the Antichrist for a one-world leader who has the reach and power to respond to such plagues to bring them under control. The pale rider will give greater power to the rider on the white horse to consolidate his global kingdom.

FINAL FORESHADOWS

As frightening as it is, the outbreak of coronavirus is not the fulfillment of the prophecies of Jesus or John. The pale rider has not yet come. The coronavirus is not a fulfillment but a frightening foreshadow, a foretaste, of what lies ahead. It's one of the first pandemics of the twenty-first century. But how can we be sure that coronavirus is not one of the plagues of Revelation?

There are several key markers. The rapture has not

occurred (the bride of Christ is still here). The tribulation period has not commenced because the Antichrist—the rider on the white horse—has not appeared to implement his peace plan that begins the tribulation. The curtain of the end times has not been raised. We're still in the time when the stage is being set. Coming events always cast their shadows before them. The days of the Apocalypse have not dawned, but we see the shadow of the pale rider all around us.

The four horsemen should serve as a warning to every person who has not fled to Jesus for refuge. Jesus can come at any moment. When He comes, He will whisk His bride to heaven—that is, anyone who has hung all their hope of life and forgiveness on the cross and the empty tomb. After the rapture, the world will be plunged into the time of tribulation and the dark days of the pale rider.

Today, when plagues strike, the search immediately begins for a vaccine or a cure. That makes sense. We have incredible health professionals and researchers that God has gifted to help us, for whom we should be thankful. Nevertheless, in the end times, when the pale rider comes forth, no cure will be found. No vaccine will be anywhere in sight. The world will succumb to an invisible enemy. Think of the panic that has come with coronavirus and then try to imagine the sheer terror that will ensue from a global pandemic as hospitals are over-run and millions die without any chance of a cure. Hope will quickly disappear. Courage will be in short supply.

Al Mohler, in addition to highlighting the severity of end-time plagues, mentioned the only place of hope and refuge: "Christians know in this case as in every other, there is no safe place to be but in Christ."[17]

I can assure you that you don't want to be on earth during the tribulation. You don't want to see the pale rider. You don't want to be left behind when Jesus comes. As terrible as these four horsemen are, they're just the preface to the tribulation. It will get much, much worse before it gets better.

But remember, the darkness of the pale rider is in sharp contrast to the bright hope of the any-moment coming of Jesus Christ. Put your trust in Jesus if you never have. He's your only refuge. If you have trusted Him as your Savior, make sure you're living for Him, sur-rendering to His will for your life each day, and sharing the good news of salvation with others.

He can come at any moment.

Make sure you're ready.

CHAPTER 7

SURVIVING A STAMPEDE

A scared world needs a fearless church.
—A. W. TOZER, *THIS WORLD*

Major John Sedgwick led a group of soldiers across the Kansas plains in 1857. They had a herd of cattle, several mule teams, and a few wagons in tow. One afternoon as they trudged across the expansive flatlands, they suddenly felt the ground shaking under their feet. They stopped dead in their tracks, and one of the experienced soldiers told Sedgwick that the tremors indicated a massive buffalo herd was approaching. Very soon they would be caught in a thundering stampede—an avalanche of hooves and horns.

The vastness of buffalo herds during that time is difficult to conceive. Herds could stretch 150 to 200 miles across. Major Sedgwick knew there was no way around the stampede. It was simply too vast. He also knew there was no way to outrun it and that they couldn't shoot all the buffalo. Sedgwick had been an officer for thirty years, but he was from Connecticut and had no idea what to do. He had never faced anything like this. With the thundering stampede approaching, Sedgwick turned pale and looked to one of his captains, Samuel Sturgis, and said, "Sam, what'll we do?"

Sturgis was an experienced soldier of the plains and had faced a stampede before, so he took over. He ordered the men to form the wagons and horses in a tight V shape and then gathered all the troops at the point of the V. At his command, as the stampede was bearing down on them, he ordered his men to fire at the point right in front of them, at the front of the herd, and not to stop. The group of petrified soldiers fired nonstop for thirty minutes. Their directed fire quickly created a heap of dead buffalo, and the herd divided, narrowly passing each side of the V without destroying the soldiers or their wagons or livestock. They were saved that day because Captain Sturgis knew what to do. He knew what to do when facing a stampede.

The question for us today is: Do we know what to do? We're facing a stampede of fear, anxiety, uncertainty, loneliness, and even depression and despair. We need to know what to do.

To help us divide the herd that's bearing down on us, we need to focus our hearts and minds on four biblical strategies that we can employ to survive this stampede and help those around us survive as well: *perspective*, *practicality*, *prayer*, and *proclamation*.

MAINTAIN PERSPECTIVE

The first essential step in surviving a stampede is maintaining a biblical perspective. It's so easy in times of chaos and confusion for our outlook to become severely skewed—to give in to stress and panic.

Most believers know there's no better place to turn in times of trouble than the book of Psalms. We instinctively turn there in turbulent times. This treasure trove of Hebrew poetry deals with every emergency and eventuality of life. The psalms span the spiritual and emotional spectrum.

Psalm 11 is one of my favorites for maintaining balance and perspective in times of trial. Please read these words carefully and thoughtfully:

> In the LORD I take refuge.
> How then can you say to me:
> "Flee like a bird to your mountain.

For look, the wicked bend their bows;
> they set their arrows against the strings
to shoot from the shadows
> at the upright in heart.
When the foundations are being destroyed,
> what can the righteous do?"

The LORD is in his holy temple;
> the LORD is on his heavenly throne.
He observes everyone on earth;
> his eyes examine them.
The LORD examines the righteous,
> but the wicked, those who love violence,
> he hates with a passion.
On the wicked he will rain
> fiery coals and burning sulfur;
> a scorching wind will be their lot.

For the LORD is righteous,
> he loves justice;
> the upright will see his face.

From these verses, we reason that David was facing the equivalent of a stampeding herd of bison that threatened to trample him. His enemies had risen up against him, and the very foundations of society were shaking beneath his feet. In that environment, David penned this psalm of trust. The lasting lesson of Psalm 11 is simple: *when the foundations are being destroyed, we need a fresh view of God and a long view of history.*

I have two simple points to develop this thought.

1. The Stampede
2. The Shelter

We begin with the stampede in verses 1–3. We can't pinpoint David's historical situation that brought forth this psalm, but based on the language of verse 2, some people think he was facing a military assault. Others believe the language is figurative. All we know for sure is that it was born out of crisis. As David wrote these words, he was surrounded by friends, but his counselors were devoid of faith. Their panicked advice to David was to head for the hills—give in to your panic and "flee like a bird to your mountain" (v. 1).

The situation David faced was so dire that he said the foundations were being destroyed. The word *foundations* refers to pillars. It's been variously translated:

- "the foundational principles of society"
- "the settled order of things"
- "the stays of society, the things upon which the culture is built"

It's a metaphor for the order of society: the established institutions; the social, moral, and civil order of the community; and the pillars upon which a house rests. When the pillars crumble, the whole house falls. It's overthrown. That's what David faced, and that's what we seem to be facing today. Foundations are crumbling right before our eyes. We live in a runaway world—a time of upheaval, uncertainty—and that's unsettling.

What can the righteous do in times like these? David told us in verses 4–7 that when the foundations are being destroyed, our shelter is a fresh view of God and a long view of history. Notice in verse 1 that David affirmed his own trust before turning to what others were saying. He opened this psalm with the words "In the LORD I take refuge." This was the foundational truth of David's life. He kept the Lord at the center of his vision. He looked at everything through this lens. The Lord was his shelter and sanctuary. When all else is moving, we go to the One who is immovable. As Proverbs 18:10 reminds us: "The name of the LORD is a fortified tower; the righteous run to it and are safe."

When everything is shifting, we go to the One who is secure. The rest of Psalm 11 gives us a fresh view of God, who is our shelter. It reminds us of three things about God.

1. *Where the Lord Sits*

The greatest thing to know when the foundations are coming apart is that God is on His throne (v. 4). Heaven has an occupied throne. It's easy to judge by appearances of the moment and believe that God has abdicated His throne. He seems so strangely silent. Trouble seems to be mushrooming unopposed.

In spite of how things may look to the world, Christians believe there's a God who sits on the throne of the universe, who is absolutely sovereign and whose ways are far above our ways. God is sovereign, and God is sufficient. God is not *almost* sovereign. God is *absolutely* sovereign. God was not caught off guard by the coronavirus pandemic. It didn't catch Him by surprise. Rather than rehearse the chaos of the world, we must rejoice in God's sovereignty.

> Your throne, O God, will last for ever and ever.
> (Psalm 45:6)

> The LORD has established His throne in the
> heavens,
> and His sovereignty rules over all. (Psalm
> 103:19 NASB)

> Our God is in heaven;
> he does whatever pleases him. (Psalm 115:3)

The word *throne* appears a great number of times in the book of Revelation; it's one of the key words in the book.[1] The structure of Revelation highlights God's sovereign rule. The scenes in Revelation ping-pong from events on earth to scenes of God's throne room in heaven. The purpose of this structure is to reassure the reader that what's happening on earth is controlled by God from His throne in heaven. God wants us to know that heaven rules even in the end times.

God is never shocked, surprised, or worried by crises or calamities. In heaven there's never panic, only plans. God is not nervously pacing the floor of heaven. The Trinity never meets in emergency session.

When the foundations are shaking, we find strength in knowing where the Lord sits.

2. What the Lord Sees

Second, we find shelter in knowing what the Lord sees (vv. 4–5). God sits on His throne; He's omnipotent (all-powerful). God sees all things; He's omniscient (all-knowing). I once heard someone ask, "Has it ever occurred to you that nothing has ever occurred to God?" That's pretty profound. God sees all and knows all.

Several English translations of Psalm 11 speak of "His eyelids" in verse 4. This pictures God squinting. Of course, God doesn't need to squint to see clearly, but the psalmist chose this imagery to emphasize that God looks closely and makes up-close examination. The point is that God sees everything. He reads the fine print. He searches every heart. He knows every thought. He sees what's happening. He examines. He tries us. He uses turbulent times to test our faith. We need to make sure we pass the test.

Knowing that God sees everything that's going on and sees to us and through us should give us comfort in difficult times. Nothing escapes His gaze.

3. What the Lord Shares

In Psalm 11:6, David transitioned to the future tense and looked ahead to the final judgment. He took us all the way to the end and reminded us that God controls the present and the future. David told us that we need to take the long view of life. The God who sees all things will judge the wicked and bring them down in the end, but the righteous will see God's face.

Notice this psalm begins and ends with "the LORD." It opens with the Lord as our refuge; it ends with the Lord as our hope. Present circumstances may be dark, but for believers, the future is magnificent. The Lord shares His presence with us. We will see His face. That's the long-term perspective we need to maintain, not as a form of escapism but as a comforting reality that we will ultimately see His face and spend eternity with Him. Whatever we face now is temporary. Our destiny is to be with Him eternally.

In his book *Muscular Faith*, Ben Patterson said,

When circumstances aren't as agreeable as I want them to be, I practice a little spiritual discipline that has managed to feed my hope and keep me in joy, nevertheless. I have a long version and a short version. Someone will ask me how I am, and I'll answer, "Other than the fact that all my sins are forgiven and that I'm going to live in heaven eternally in the joy of God, I'm not doing too well." The look on the questioner's face always amuses me. That, and the little irony of saying I'm not doing too well in the face of such magnificent aspects, usually lifts the cloud a bit. That's the long version. The short version is simply to answer, "I'm fundamentally sound."[2]

I like that. Even in the face of unpleasant, uncertain circumstances, I can say, "I'm fundamentally sound" because of my past and my future. Christ has forgiven all my sins and promised me a heavenly home in His presence. I'm safe and sound.

The first thing we need to do when facing a stampede is gain and maintain a biblical perspective.

TAKE PRACTICAL STEPS

The second thing we need to do in a stampede is take practical, proactive steps to protect ourselves, our families, and our neighbors. In the midst of a stampede, many people can get trampled, especially the most needy and vulnerable among us. Every believer needs to be on the lookout for those who need help, encouragement, and assistance.

We have to remember that we aren't the first generation to face a perilous plague. Deadly plagues have ravaged the planet for centuries. The church of Jesus Christ has had to navigate plagues many times throughout history. In those perilous times, the church rose to the occasion to sacrifice for others and to serve them.

Martin Luther was a theologian and the father of the Protestant Reformation, but he also had some practical advice that is applicable to today's pastors and communities dealing with the coronavirus pandemic. The deadly bubonic plague hit Martin Luther's town of Wittenberg, Germany, in 1527, setting off a shock wave of panic. Many drastic actions were taken, including the closing of Wittenberg University. (That should sound familiar.) Remember, the bubonic plague wiped out somewhere between 30 and 60 percent of Europe's population.

In the face of the plague, Luther was urged to flee, even by many of his best friends and supporters. Believers in Germany debated how they should respond. Luther was besieged by pastors who wanted to know his thoughts on dealing with the plague and wanted him to make a statement. In response, Luther produced a paper titled "Whether One May Flee from a Deadly Plague" or, as the printer titled it, "Whether one may flee death." Luther wrote,

> I shall ask God mercifully to protect us. Then I shall fumigate, help purify the air, administer medicine, and take it. I shall avoid places and persons where my presence is not needed in order not to become contaminated and thus perchance inflict and pollute others, and so cause their death as a result of my negligence. If God should wish to take me, he will surely find me and I have done what he has expected of me and so I am not responsible for either my own death or the death of others. If my neighbor needs me, however, I shall not avoid place or person but will go freely, as stated above. See, this is such a God-fearing faith because it is neither brash nor foolhardy and does not tempt God.[3]

This text drips with prudence, wisdom, and practicality. It reads like scriptural, sixteenth-century CDC guidelines. We could call it prudent boldness. God wants us to trust in Him, but He also honors real-world, concrete steps to love our neighbors as ourselves. He wants us to do all we can to protect ourselves and others. God never blesses foolish, reckless behavior.

When crisis strikes, you and I need to be like the four men who brought to Jesus their paralyzed friend on a stretcher and lowered him down through a roof (Mark 2:1–12). These men were sacrificial, bold, and creative. When they couldn't get into the house through the door, they carried their friend to the roof, dug a hole through the thatch, and lowered him at Jesus' feet. They stopped at nothing to minister to their friend and bring him to Jesus. In turbulent times we need to match their efforts to care for those around us who need the Savior's touch.

Concerning reaching out and loving and helping others in need, Luther called believers to look upon people in need as though they were Jesus.

What would you do if it was Jesus? This I well know, that if it were Christ or his mother who were laid low by illness everybody would be so solicitous and would gladly become a servant or helper. Everyone would want to be bold and fearless; nobody would flee but everyone would come running. . . . If you wish to serve Christ and to wait on him, very well, you have your sick neighbor close at hand. Go to him and serve him, and you will surely find Christ in him.[4]

If Christians adopted that attitude, think of how drastically it would change our ministry to others at all times, but especially in times of crisis and calamity. Let's ask God to help us see our friends and neighbors as Jesus sees them. To love our neighbors as ourselves. To love them like Jesus and on behalf of Jesus.

KEEP PRAYING

The late Ray Stedman served as pastor of Peninsula Bible Church in Palo Alto, California, for many years. He related a story he heard from a seasoned mariner who navigated his ship through surging, stormy seas throughout a long career. The mariner told of one particularly perilous storm when he didn't know if anyone would make it back to shore.

"Yes," the old mariner sighed, "the Lord heard the voices of many strangers that night."

As things seem to be spiraling out of control, I believe God is hearing the voices of many strangers. One of those voices might be yours. In the midst of the confusion and chaos in today's climate, are you turning to the Lord more often than ever before? If so, know that you are not alone. But most importantly, know that God hears you and that He loves you.[5]

In recent days I'm sure we've all sensed a need to take a knee in prayer like never before. As we navigate the corona crisis, few things are more important than our prayer lives. We need to turn our panic into prayer. Prayer is a powerful resource at all times but especially when facing a stampede. It has been said, "You can do more than pray after you've prayed, but you can't do more than pray until you've prayed."[6]

From Genesis to Revelation, the Scriptures are filled with prayers and petitions to the Lord. Prayer must be part of our daily lives. Prayer is an expression of our dependence on God. All the Greek words in the New Testament that are translated *prayer*, *petition*, or *supplication* carry the basic meaning of asking for something. When we turn to the Lord, we worship and adore Him, but the real essence of prayer is asking God for what we need. We come to Him because we are needy, and He is all-sufficient.

When we face a stampede, we need to pray and pray often. We need to have rich, personal prayer lives, but we also should pray with our spouses, our families, and our friends. Linking our faith with others is a key to surviving a stampede. There are many things to pray for and about, but here are a few key topics to bring to the Lord:

- Pray for protection for our families, friends, and people around the world.
- Pray for containment of today's virus as well as those we will experience in the future.
- Pray for our president, vice president, governors, legislators, and health professionals.
- Pray for the economy and for those who have lost jobs.
- Pray that we will maintain our joy.
- Pray for love for our neighbors.
- Pray for peace that passes all understanding.

Remember the timeless words from the book of Philippians: "Do not be anxious about anything, but in every situation, by prayer and petition, with thanksgiving, present your requests to God. And the peace of God, which transcends all understanding, will guard your hearts and your minds in Christ Jesus" (4:6–7). Paul called us to pray, but notice that he was talking about a *thankful* prayer. The words "with thanksgiving" are key. Grateful prayer brings peace in the middle of the stampede of anxious, fearful thoughts that threaten to overwhelm us. Thankful prayer sucks the oxygen out of anxiety and fear.

Thankful prayer produces peace.

It separates the stampede.

PROCLAIM THE GOSPEL

A fourth key strategy to employ in a stampede is boldly proclaiming the gospel. After all, in a stampede we can't think only about ourselves. We have to look out for others who may be in the path of the oncoming crisis. Of course, we need to be faithful ambassadors for Christ and the gospel at all times. Yet when times of crisis shake the world, many people have a greater openness to the claims of Christ and the gospel. People spend more time thinking about deeper issues. We need to make the most of these opportunities. At some point the window will close; people will slowly go back to normal, and indifference will once again fill their hearts.

Charles Spurgeon, speaking in 1866 amid a cholera outbreak in London, issued this charge to his fellow pastors and all other Christians:

> Now is the time for all of you who love souls. You
> may see men more alarmed than they are already;

and if they should be, mind that you avail your-selves of the opportunity of doing them good. You have the Balm of Gilead; when their wounds smart, pour it in. You know of Him who died to save; tell them of Him. Lift high the cross before their eyes. Tell them that God became man that man might be lifted to God. Tell them of Calvary, and its groans, and cries, and sweat of blood. Tell them of Jesus hanging on the cross to save sinners. Tell them that: "There is life for a look at the Crucified One." Tell them that he is able to save to the uttermost all them that come unto God by him. Tell them that he is able to save even at the eleventh hour, and to say to the dying thief, "Today shalt thou be with me in Paradise."[7]

Times of upheaval provide unique opportunities to hold out the gospel.

Charles Thomas Studd, known as C. T. Studd, was a famous missionary from England to China, India, and Africa in the nineteenth century. On one occasion when he was back in England, Studd was burdened for his family and looked for opportunities to win them to Christ. During that time, he was invited to speak in Wales, and one of his cousins who lived in the area asked him to stay with her and her husband while he was there. He accepted the invitation with one condition: that she would come to hear him speak. She agreed.

In the course of his message at one of the meetings in Wales, Studd said, "True religion is like the smallpox. If you get it, you give it to others, and it spreads." On the way back to her home, Studd's cousin told him she thought it was awful and disgusting for him to compare the gospel to smallpox. That led to a long conversation about the gospel.

When they arrived at her house, she served Studd some hot cocoa and tried to converse with him. As she talked to him, he kept ignoring her. After this went on for a while, she got quite annoyed. "Well," he said, "that is exactly how you are treating God, who is holding out eternal life to you." The arrow pierced her heart.

Studd left the next morning and returned to London. Two days later he received this telegram from his cousin: "Got the smallpox—badly."[8]

The same should be true of us, but we could substitute coronavirus for smallpox. The gospel of Jesus Christ is like coronavirus. When you get it, you give it to others, and it spreads. In that sense, may God help all of us get a case of "spiritual virus" . . . and to get it badly.

May it spread to many so they can escape the stampede.

STOP THE STAMPEDE

In his book *Fearless*, Max Lucado related a story from March 3, 1943, when bomb sirens pierced the air in London, England, causing people to stop whatever they were doing and seek shelter. The unfamiliar sound of new antiaircraft guns in the distance caused many people to panic as they raced to the Bethnal Green Underground Station, which was filling up quickly.

> Trouble began when a rush of safety seekers reached the stairwell entrance at the same time. A woman carrying a baby lost her footing on one of the nineteen uneven steps leading down from the street. Her stumble interrupted the oncoming flow, causing a domino of others to tumble on top of her. Within seconds, hundreds of horrified people were thrown together, piling up like laundry in a basket. . . . The chaos lasted for less than a quarter of an hour. The disentangling of bodies took until midnight. In the end 173 men, women, and children died.
>
> No bombs had been dropped.
>
> Fusillades didn't kill people. Fear did.
>
> Fear loves a good stampede. Fear's payday is blind panic, unfounded disquiet, and sleepless nights. Fear's been making a good living lately.[9]

Sadly, he's right. Fear has been making quite a living lately. Maybe it's been making a good living off you as you live in fear. Fear about your future. Fear about your family. Fear about your finances. Fear about a potentially fatal illness. If so, why not commit to stop paying fear? Why not stop the stampede in your life?

Start unloading all your spiritual ammunition at the center of the stampede. Fire away by applying God's truth to your life, and watch the stampeding herd separate as you stand firm and fearless because of our great God and the power of His might.

CHAPTER 8

THE UNIVERSAL VIRUS . . .
AND ITS CURE

All of us . . . are born infected
with the contagion of sin.

—John Calvin, Institutes of
the Christian Religion

There are some things we don't like to think about. There's something common to our humanity that has a strong aversion to certain topics and activities. We avoid them like the plague (pun intended). Things like public speaking, going to the doctor, losing a job, family conflict, paying taxes, getting a root canal, and, of course, the worst of all, death. The list may vary a bit from person to person, but we all have things we avoid thinking about.

One thing that would make most people's list of top things not to think about is disease, a deadly virus. After all, who wants to spend day after day for months on end hearing about a virus, thinking about a virus, and avoiding a virus? Nobody.

Yet when the coronavirus reached pandemic status, that's what we all did for weeks (and predicting for months as of this writing). We were all preoccupied with that contagion, consumed with it, and obsessed by the outbreak all across the globe. Due to circumstances beyond our control, we were forced to think about something we don't usually spend any time considering: a tiny virus.

We've all been constrained to confront an unsavory reality.

There's another subject that most people avoid like the plague. It's probably even more unpopular than a virus. What is it? Sin. Humans don't like thinking about sin. Especially their own. I don't, and you don't. Spending too much time focused on sin can be downright depressing. Who wants to examine faults, failures, and flaws? We'd rather think of ourselves in a more positive light. Sin has never been a popular topic, and that couldn't be more true today. Even many churches steer clear of ever mentioning the "S" word for fear of offending someone.

But just as the COVID-19 pandemic forced us all to focus on something we would rather dodge, so it has steered many of us to take stock of our lives and to think about where we stand with God. Times of crisis, while trying, can reap great benefits for those who will use them for reflection and reexamination. When life slowed down significantly for people at the beginning of 2020, there was plenty of time to stop and think about things that matter most. More opportunities to think honestly and openly about sin and our need for forgiveness.

Viruses and sin. Two things we avoid. Two things many more people are thinking about much more than usual. Two things that are more alike than you might think.

SIN GOES VIRAL

Sin is compared to many things in the Bible. Sin is like leaven or yeast in that it spreads and permeates. Sin is like leprosy since it contaminates and is incurable. Sin is like seed that, once it's planted, brings a bitter harvest. Sin is also like a disease that needs to be cured. Jesus said, "It is not the healthy who need a doctor, but the sick. I have not come to call the righteous, but sinners" (Mark 2:17).

With this picture in mind, let's look at a few of the comparisons and contrasts between coronavirus and sin and then open our hearts and minds to what God wants to teach us.

Comparisons

There are several interesting parallels between coronavirus and sin.

Like a virus, sin is invisible.

Like a virus, sin has symptoms. Viruses normally have outward symptoms. Sin always has terrible symptoms.

Like a virus, sin is inward. It comes from deep within.

Like a virus, sin is real. It can be verified and diagnosed. As Reinhold Niebuhr once said "The doctrine of original sin is the only Christian doctrine that is empirically verifiable."[1]

Like a virus, sin weakens us and separates us from others.

Like many viruses, sin is deadly. Sin brings spiritual death or separation from God. "The wages of sin is death" (Romans 6:23).

Like a virus, sin spreads. It's a universal pandemic. It passes from parent to child and person to person.

Like many viruses, sin has no human cure. We can't cure the sin virus by our good deeds, church attendance, religious rituals, penance, or prayers. The Bible is clear that no amount of human effort can remove one sin. We're powerless to cure ourselves (Romans 5:6).

Contrasts

There are also important differences between a virus and sin. Unlike a virus that affects only a limited number of people, sin is carried by everyone. Even in the worst pandemic, many people escape infection. The devastating Spanish flu infected about half the people on earth in the early twentieth century. Not so with sin. No amount of social distancing or handwashing can spare you. Everyone has it. Young and old, rich and poor, educated and uneducated, wise and foolish. The infection rate is 100 percent. No one is immune. There's no vaccine. "For all have sinned and fall short of the glory of God" (Romans 3:23). The German theologian Dietrich Bonhoeffer wrote in his book *Creation and Fall* that we live in a "fallen and falling world."[2]

Unlike a virus, with sin no one is asymptomatic. Some people walk around with coronavirus and have no discernible symptoms. Sin, on the other hand, always shows itself in our attitudes and actions. You can't hide the ugly symptoms.

Unlike a virus, sin brings the judgment of God. A virus may kill the body, but sin slays the soul.

Unlike a virus, with sin there's a 100 percent cure rate with the proper prescription.

Unlike a virus, sin can be cured forever. That's the good news for all of us infected with the pandemic of sin. There's hope. There's a cure. It works every time.

COMPLETELY CURED

Way back in June 1965, the month before I turned six years old, I sat with my parents in the living room of our small house and watched Billy Graham on a thirteen-inch black-and-white television as he preached at one of his crowded evangelistic crusades in a large outdoor stadium. The crusade was on local television four nights in a row. It was the final night. As always, Graham was faithful to proclaim the gospel of Jesus Christ and offer an invitation to all who would receive Christ as their substitute. That evening, when he passionately appealed to the audience to accept Jesus Christ and His forgiveness of sin, I went to my room and got down on my knees. With a simple, childlike faith, I received Jesus and His gracious offer of eternal life. In its simplest terms, even as a young boy, I recognized that I had a problem I could never remedy on my own. I knew I needed a Savior. I needed a Substitute. I needed a pardon for my sins. I needed a cure for my disease.

On one occasion, likening sin to a deadly virus, Billy Graham put it like this:

> Sin is the most serious thing man will ever deal with. Sin is a spiritual virus that invades our whole being. It makes us morally and spiritually weak. It's a deadly disease that infects every part of us: our body, our mind, our emotions, our relationships, our motives—absolutely everything. We don't have the strength on our own to overcome its power. . . .
>
> Sin is the great clogger, and the blood of Christ is the great cleanser. We don't need to be crippled any longer by the disease of sin because God has provided the cure. "The blood of Jesus Christ . . . cleanses us from all sin" (1 John 1:7 [NKJV]).[3]

With all that's going on in our world today, maybe you've been thinking more about your spiritual condition and about the life to come. Jesus is the cure for the plague infecting your soul. Jesus is the way to God and heaven. Jesus took the full effect of the sin virus for us through His death and resurrection. He took it all. Jesus will cleanse your sins if you will receive Him as your substitute.

There's a little rhyme I heard years ago that sums up the good news of the gospel:

LIFE IS SHORT, DEATH IS SURE;
SIN THE CAUSE, CHRIST THE CURE.[4]

YOU HAVE TO TAKE IT

When I was a boy, a well-known Bible teacher from Kansas City named Dr. Walter Wilson used to come speak at our church. I always enjoyed his clear, compelling messages. He was a medical doctor the Lord used to teach the Bible and share the gospel with people everywhere he went. There are dozens of amazing stories about his encounters with various people and his boldness to communicate the gospel to them in simple language.

One such story occurred when Dr. Wilson was preaching in a church on a Sunday evening. In his message, Dr. Wilson compared sin to a disease or virus. He detailed all the ways sin and a virus are alike. As he brought the message to a close, he wanted the people to understand the cure for sin. He pointed out that when we get sick we visit the doctor and get a prescription to cure our illness.

He then asked, "Will having the medicine do you any good?"[5]

There was a long period of uncomfortable silence. Finally, a young man in the back pew shouted out, "Not unless you take it!"

Dr. Wilson said, "That's right. It won't do you any good if you never take it."

I realize this story is very simple, but it does drive home the essential message that the truth of the gospel must be personally received. The healing power of the gospel must be taken to have effect. As life-giving and liberating as the gospel is, you have to receive it personally to get its benefits. You have to take it.

Have you taken it?

Let's say, God forbid, that you or I get the coronavirus. Maybe you've already had it. But what if you contract it or some other virus months or even years from now, and as the symptoms are worsening you find out that a cure has been discovered. It's a sure thing. It works 100 percent of the time. And just to make sure everyone has access to the cure, the government is offering it free of charge to anyone who needs it. All you have to do is get a prescription from your doctor, get a friend or relative to pick up the prescription at the nearest pharmacy, and bring it to you.

Would you take it?

Of course you would. Who would be foolish enough to refuse a fail-safe cure, especially one that's totally free? Yet that's what millions of people do when they refuse the free offer of eternal life and forgiveness through Jesus Christ. There are undoubtedly many reasons for this. Maybe they just keep putting it off, waiting for a later time. Maybe they don't really believe the illness is fatal. Maybe they hope they can find another cure. Maybe they think they can cure it on their own. Excuses abound.

The actor W. C. Fields was well-known as an agnostic. Not long before his death, a friend visited Fields in the hospital and was surprised to find him flipping through a Bible. Asked what he was doing with a Bible, Fields replied, "I'm looking for loopholes."[6] Nice try.

But there are no loopholes, only a Lord. The only way to be cured and cleansed of sin is through the Lord Jesus Christ.

There are no magic words that bring salvation; it's an issue of the heart. But a simple prayer like this one, if said sincerely, will reach the ear of God and move His heart to save you.

Father, I know I'm a sinner. I know I cannot save myself. I need a Savior. I believe Jesus is the Savior I need. I believe He died on the cross in my place and rose from the grave on the third day. Please forgive me of my sins—past, present, and future. I trust in Him and receive Him now as my personal Savior who paid the penalty for my sins. Thank You for bringing me into Your family and making me Your child forever.

HAND TO HAND

Henri Nouwen was a Dutch Catholic priest. Years ago in Germany he met a group of trapeze artists called the Flying Rodleighs and became a friend of their leader, whom the group was named after. Nouwen was fascinated by the athleticism and artistry of the trapeze flyers.

One day when Nouwen was sitting with Rodleigh talking about flying, Rodleigh said,

"As a flyer, I must have complete trust in my catcher. The public might think that I am the great star of the trapeze, but the real star is Joe, my catcher. He has to be there for me with split-second precision and grab me out of the air as I come to him in the long jump."
"How does it work?" I asked. "The secret," Rodleigh said, "is that the flyer does nothing and the catcher does everything." . . .

"You do nothing!" I said, surprised. "Nothing," Rodleigh repeated. "The worst thing the flyer can do is to try to catch the catcher. I am not supposed to catch Joe. It's Joe's task to catch me. If I grabbed Joe's wrists, I might break them, or he might break mine, and that would be the end for both of us. A flyer must fly, and a catcher must catch, and the flyer must trust, with outstretched arms, that his catcher will be there for him."[7]

If you've never done so, reach out your hand and let the Lord do His work of catching. The same hand that reached out to save sinking Peter will reach out to you. He will touch you, He will catch you, and you will live.

ACKNOWLEDGMENTS

I thank God for the privilege to do what I love every day—study, teach, and write about His inspired, infallible Word. I'm mindful that few people get to do what they love every day, so I gratefully acknowledge God's kindness to me and never want to take it for granted. My acknowledgment of Him eclipses all else in importance.

At the center of all I do, other than the Lord, is my wife, Cheryl, who has made my life easy and enjoyable for over three decades. She freely gives me herself and her time, and with that I get her wisdom and insight, which I highly value. For our almost thirty-four years as marriage and ministry partners, God has been better to us than we would have ever dreamed. This book is another expression of God's grace to us, for which we give thanks.

ACKNOWLEDGMENTS

As events continued to unfold with the coronavirus crisis, the folks at W Publishing Group worked tirelessly and with excellence to expedite the release of this book. That put a great deal of extra pressure on the editing team, but they made it look easy and helped me look much better than I otherwise would. I'm grateful they share my vision of helping people connect current events to biblical prophecy and then live in light of that truth. Their excellent work was spearheaded by publisher Damon Reiss and senior acquisitions editor Kyle Olund. Additional thanks go to associate publisher Stephanie Newton and senior editor Dawn Hollomon for rallying the troops coordinating such a crazy publishing schedule.

Of course, there's much more to a book than its writing and release. Thanks to all who've labored to promote, market, and increase the reach of this book. My daughter-in-law, Natalee, is the key to the team that keeps my social media in order and assists me with marketing. I appreciate her willingness and readiness to help her technologically challenged father-in-law. She never makes me feel dim or outdated.

I have the privilege of being represented by William K. Jensen, who is also a very close, dear friend. I greatly value Bill's input, wisdom, and friendship. God has blessed and honored our relationship over the years as we have sought to honor Him. Bill is always available to offer a listening ear and a valuable voice. I pray that God continues to give us the creativity and opportunity to produce books that point people to Jesus and His coming.

The elders and members of Faith Bible Church, where I serve as senior pastor, have been and continue to be an anchor in my life. Their faithful support and constant encouragement energize me to fulfill God's calling on my life with joy. No pastor ever served a better church.

May the Lord use all our combined efforts, meager as they are, to bring abundant glory to His name and animate us to be ready when the trumpet sounds.

—Dr. Mark Hitchcock
Edmond, Oklahoma—April 2020

NOTES

Preface: What in the World Is Going On?

1. Julie Zauzmer and Sarah Pulliam Bailey, "This Is Not the End of the World, According to Christians Who Study the End of the World," *The Washington Post*, March 17, 2020, https://www.washingtonpost.com /religion/2020/03/17/not-end-of-the-world-coronavirus -bible-prophecy/.

2. Albert Mohler, "Coronavirus Spreads in China as Government Quarantines 25 Million People: Echoes of Plagues Past, Present, and Future," AlbertMohler.com, January 24, 2020, https://albertmohler.com/2020/01/24 /briefing-1-24-20.

Chapter 1: Corona Fever

1. *Coronavirus disease 2019* (or COVID-19 for short) is the official name given by the World Health Organization. According to the Centers for Disease Control and Prevention, "There are many types of human coronaviruses including some that commonly cause

mild upper-respiratory tract illnesses. COVID-19 is a new disease, caused by a novel (or new) coronavirus that has not previously been seen in humans" (https://www .cdc.gov/coronavirus/2019-ncov/faq.html#anchor _1584386215012). Throughout the book, I will refer to this disease using the generic term *coronavirus*.

2. Ben Zimmer, "'Black Swan': A Rare Disaster, Not as Rare as Once Believed," *The Wall Street Journal*, March 19, 2020, https://www.wsj.com/articles/black -swan-a-rare-disaster-not-as-rare-as-once-believed -11584645612.

3. Ed Yong, "How the Pandemic Will End," *The Atlantic*, March 25, 2020, https://www.theatlantic.com/health /archive/2020/03/how-will-coronavirus-end/608719/.

4. This list was adapted from an email on April 2, 2020, from my friend Ed Hindson, Dean Emeritus and Distinguished Professor of Religion, School of Divinity, Liberty University. He gave me permission to use it.

5. Rami Ayyub, "Under Coronavirus Lockdown, Armageddon Is Like the End of the World," *U.S. News & World Report*, March 17, 2020, https://www .usnews.com/news/world/articles/2020-03-17"/under -coronavirus-lockdown-armageddon-is-like -the-end-of-the-world.

6. Elizabeth Dias, "The Apocalypse as an 'Unveiling': What Religion Teaches Us About the End Times," *New York Times*, April 2, 2020, https://www.nytimes .com/2020/04/02/us/coronavirus-apocalypse-religion .html.

7. Dias, "The Apocalypse."

8. Joel C. Rosenberg, "Coronavirus Pandemic Is a Wake Up Call: Exclusive Joshua Fund Poll," The Joshua Fund, March 2020, https://www.joshuafund.com/learn/news -article/coronavirus_pandemic_is_a_wake_up_call _exclusive_joshua_fund_poll.

9. Paul Bedard, "Poll: 29% See Biblical 'Last Days,' 44% Say Virus Is God's 'Wake-up Call,'" *Washington Examiner*, March 31, 2020, https://www.washingtonexaminer.com /washington-secrets/poll-29-see-biblical-last-days-44 -say-virus-is-gods-wake-up-call.

10. Philip De Courcy, *Take Cover: Finding Peace in God's Protection* (Washington, DC: Salem Books, 2018), 67.

11. De Courcy, *Take Cover*, 68.

12. Max Lucado, *When Christ Comes* (Nashville: Word Publishing, 1999), vii.

Chapter 2: The Times of the Signs

1. Adapted from David Jeremiah, *The Book of Signs* (Nashville: W Publishing, 2019), ix.

2. Thomas Ice and Timothy Demy, *The Truth about the Signs of the Times* (Eugene, OR: Harvest House Publishers, 2005), 10.

3. Bryan Walsh, "Covid-19: The History of Pandemics," BBC Future, March 25, 2020, https://www.bbc.com /future/article/20200325-covid-19-the-history-of -pandemics.

4. Larry Elliott, "Gordon Brown calls for global government to tackle coronavirus," *The Guardian*,

March 26, 2020, https://www.theguardian.com /politics/2020/mar/26/gordon-brown-calls-for -global-government-to-tackle-coronavirus.

5. Philip De Courcy, *Take Cover: Finding Peace in God's Protection* (Washington, DC: Salem Books, 2018), 68.

Chapter 3: Plagues—Past and Present

1. "Quote by Winston S. Churchill," Goodreads, https:// www.goodreads.com/quotes/69209-the-farther -backward-you-can-look-the-farther-forward-you.

2. *Merriam-Webster.com Dictionary*, s.v. "pestilence," accessed April 5, 2020, https://www.merriam-webster .com/dictionary/pestilence.

3. *Merriam-Webster.com Dictionary*, s.v. "plague," accessed April 5, 2020, https://www.merriam-webster.com /dictionary/plague.

4. Laura Spinney, *Pale Rider: The Spanish Flu of 1918 and How It Changed the World* (New York: PublicAffairs, 2017), 13.

5. William C. Shiel Jr., "Medical Definition of Epidemic," MedicineNet, reviewed on December 4, 2018, https:// www.medicinenet.com/script/main/art.asp?articlekey =3273.

6. "'Pandemic' vs 'Epidemic': How They Overlap and How They Differ" Merriam-Webster.com, March 12, 2020, https://www.merriam-webster.com/words-at-play /epidemic-vs-pandemic-difference.

7. Joel C. Rosenberg, "What Does the Bible Teach About Pestilence, Plagues and Global Pandemics?", The Joshua

Fund, March 2020, https://www.joshuafund.com/images
/blog_uploads/FACTSHEET-BibleAndPandemics
_BRANDED_v2.pdf.

8. Bryan Walsh, "Covid-19: The History of Pandemics,"
BBC Future, March 25, 2020, https://www.bbc.com
/future/article/20200325-covid-19-the-history-of
-pandemics.

9. Felix Salmon, "How Pandemics Are Worse Than
Wars," Axios, April 2, 2020, https://www.axios.com
/coronavirus-pandemic-worse-than-war-8cada36c
-3deb-4335-8863-0fc3b394bbcf.html.

10. Nicholas LePan, "Visualizing the History of
Pandemics," Visual Capitalist, March 14, 2020, https://
www.visualcapitalist.com/history-of-pandemics
-deadliest/.

11. "Situation Report - 77," World Health Organization,
accessed April 6, 2020, https://www.who.int
/emergencies/diseases/novel-coronavirus-2019
/situation-reports/.

12. Felix Salmon, "How Pandemics Are Worse Than Wars."

13. Swinney, *Pale Rider*, 23.

14. Swinney, *Pale Rider*, 199.

15. Swinney, *Pale Rider*, 228.

16. John M. Barry, *The Great Influenza: The Epic Story
of the Greatest Plague in History* (New York: Penguin
Books, 2005), 4–5.

17. Walsh, "Covid-19: The History of Pandemics."

18. Quoted by Joel C. Rosenberg, "What Does the Bible
Teach About Pestilence?"

Chapter 4: Is Coronavirus the Judgment of God?

1. Laura Spinney, *Pale Rider: The Spanish Flu of 1918 and How It Changed the World* (New York: PublicAffairs, 2017), 79.

2. Spinney, *Pale Rider*, 78.

3. Jennifer LeClaire, "Is Deadly Ebola Outbreak the First Bowl of 'Revelation' Judgment?" Charisma News, August 8, 2014, http://www.charismanews.com/opinion /watchman-on-the-wall/44953-is-deadly-ebola-outbreak -the-first-bowl-of-revelation-judgment.

4. Leonardo Blair, "'This Could Be Bad,' CDC Official Warns of Inevitable Coronavirus Spread in US," The Christian Post, February 26, 2020, https://www .christianpost.com/news/this-could-be-bad-cdc-official -warns-of-inevitable-coronavirus-spread-in-us.html.

5. "Israeli Rabbi: Coronavirus Outbreak Is Divine Punishment for Gay Pride Parades," The Times of Israel, March 8, 2020, https://www.timesofisrael.com/israeli -rabbi-blames-coronavirus-outbreak-on-gay-pride-parades/.

6. Max Lucado, "Loved by a Trustworthy God," UpWords, January 23, 2020, https://www.oneplace.com/devotionals /upwords-with-max-lucado/upwords-week-of-august-12 -18-11654901.html.

7. R. Kent Hughes, *Luke*, vol. 2 (Wheaton, IL: Crossway, 1998), 80.

8. Hughes, *Luke*, 80.

9. Darrell L. Bock, *Luke 9:51–24:53*, Baker Exegetical Commentary on the New Testament, ed. Moises Silva (Grand Rapids, MI: Baker Books, 1996), 1206.

10. Hughes, *Luke*, 80.
11. Quoted in Philip Graham Ryken, *Luke*, vol. 2, Reformed Expository Commentary, ed. Richard D. Phillips and Philip Graham Ryken (Phillipsburg, NJ: P&R Publishing, 2009), 8.
12. Timothy Keller, *Gospel in Life Study Guide: Grace Changes Everything* (Grand Rapids, MI: Zondervan, 2010), 28.
13. Quoted in Lauren Green, "Is the Coronavirus God's Judgment? Pastor Weighs In," Fox News, March 13, 2020, https://www.foxnews.com/faith-value s/coronavirus-update-christian-question-god-judgment.
14. Warren Peel, "A Christian Response to the Corona Virus," Banner of Truth, March 3, 2020, https:// banneroftruth.org/us/resources/articles/2020/a -christian-response-to-the-corona-virus/.

Chapter 5: Pestilence in Various Places

1. Max Lucado, *Fearless* (Nashville: Thomas Nelson, 2009), 153.
2. Philip De Courcy, *Take Cover: Finding Peace in God's Protection* (Washington, D.C: Salem Books, 2018), 71.
3. De Courcy, *Take Cover*, 74.
4. De Courcy, *Take Cover*, 71.
5. There are four main views of the chronology of the events in the Olivet Discourse: (1) Preterists (from a Latin word meaning "past") hold that the entire sermon is about the events of AD 70 and the destruction of Jerusalem and the temple. The main basis for their view

is Jesus' statement in Matthew 24:34, "Truly I tell you, this generation will certainly not pass away until all these things have happened." Preterists contend that the entire prophecy had to be fulfilled within the generation that heard Jesus' words. I believe Jesus was speaking about the generation who will witness the beginning of the birth pains in the future tribulation. That the generation won't pass away until all has been fulfilled. The preterist view is difficult to maintain in light of the clear statement about Christ's coming on the clouds to rescue and gather His people (Matthew 24:29–31). Furthermore, the events of AD 70 were a judgment on Jerusalem, not a rescue as Jesus predicted. (2) Others, possibly a majority of scholars and commentators, believe the sermon had a historic fulfillment in AD 70, but that the destruction of Jerusalem at that time serves as a preview of the distant days of the end times. This view is sometimes referred to as a "double fulfillment" and is difficult to support in light of the numerous parallels between Matthew 24 and Revelation 6. (3) Another view is that the events of Matthew 24:4–14 are unfolding and intensifying in this present age. The image of birth pains argues against this view. Birth pains point to a fulfillment that comes soon after the pains begin, not after a prolonged period of time. (4) The fourth view, the one that I hold, is that Matthew 24 refers to events that are still future, that will transpire during the final time of tribulation just before the return of Jesus to earth.

6. Patrick Frye, "Franklin Graham: Ebola Virus May Be Part of Bible End Times Prophecy Predicting End of The World," The Inquisitr, September 11, 2014, http://www.inquisitr.com/1467882/franklin-graham-ebola-virus-may-be-part-of-bible-end-times-prophecy-predicting-end-of-the-world/.

7. Todd Hampson, "COVID-19: How Should We Respond?" ToddHampson.com, accessed April 2, 2020, http://toddhampson.com/how-should-we-respond-to-the-coronavirus/. This was the view of my dear friend and mentor, the late Dr. John F. Walvoord. He saw the prophecies of Matthew 24:4–14 as general signs that mark the progress of this present age and "indicate that the end of the age is approaching." He observed: "In a very real sense these signs have been a general part of the entire history of the inter-advent age. There have been many false religious leaders or false messiahs through the centuries. War, famine, and pestilence are still with us; indeed, we are being warned of 'super viruses' that could be resistant to any known treatment. There is some evidence that there is an increase in earthquakes." However, Dr. Walvoord did acknowledge that the birth pains in Matthew 24 will "characterize worldwide events during the first half of the coming tribulation period." John F. Walvoord and Charles H. Dyer, *Matthew*, ed. Philip E. Rawley (Chicago: Moody Publishers, 2013), 318–21.

8. Anne Graham Lotz, "Is the Coronavirus a Sign of the

End?" Anne Graham Lotz Angel Ministries, March 13, 2020, https://www.annegrahamlotz.org/2020/03/13/is-the-coronavirus-a-sign-of-the-end/.

9. John F. MacArthur, *Matthew 24–28* (Chicago: Moody Press, 1989), 15.

10. Warren W. Wiersbe, *The Bible Exposition Commentary*, vol. 1 (Wheaton, IL: Victor Books, 1989), 87.

11. Wiersbe, *Bible Exposition*, 261.

12. John F. MacArthur, *The Second Coming* (Wheaton, IL: Crossway Books, 1999), 81.

13. MacArthur, *Second Coming*, 89.

14. Lucado, *Fearless*, 157.

Chapter 6: Thundering Hoofbeats of the Pale Rider

1. Billy Graham, *Approaching Hoofbeats* (Waco, TX: Word Books, 1983), 9, 12.

2. Max Lucado, *Fearless* (Nashville: Thomas Nelson, 2009), 155.

3. John F. Walvoord, *The Revelation of Jesus Christ* (Chicago: Moody Press, 1966), 129.

4. Robert L. Thomas, *Revelation 1–7: An Exegetical Commentary* (Chicago: Moody Press, 1992), 436.

5. Charles R. Swindoll, *Insights on Revelation* (Grand Rapids, MI: Zondervan, 2011), 111.

6. Billy Graham, *Storm Warning* (Nashville: Thomas Nelson, 2010), 237.

7. John F. MacArthur, *Revelation 12–22* (Chicago: Moody Press, 1999), 136.

8. Thomas, *Revelation 1–7*, 439.

9. Henry M. Morris, *The Revelation Record* (Wheaton, IL: Tyndale House, 1983), 118.

10. John F. MacArthur, *Revelation 1–11* (Chicago: Moody Press, 1999), 184. See also: David Jeremiah, *Escape the Coming Night* (Dallas: Word Publishing, 1997), 120–21, and Grant R. Osborne, *Revelation*, Baker Exegetical Commentary on the New Testament, ed. Moises Silva (Grand Rapids, MI: Baker Academic, 2002), 283. Osborne seems to view the wild beasts of the earth as the birds that will feed on the carrion described further in Revelation 19:17–18, 21.

11. Adrian Rogers, *Unveiling the End Times in Our Time* (Nashville: Broadman & Holman, 2004), 90.

12. "Zoonotic Diseases," Centers for Disease Control and Prevention, accessed March 26, 2020, https://www.cdc .gov/onehealth/basics/zoonotic-diseases.html.

13. Albert Mohler, "Coronavirus Spreads in China as Government Quarantines 25 Million People: Echoes of Plagues Past, Present, and Future," AlbertMohler.com, January 24, 2020, https://albertmohler.com/2020/01/24 /briefing-1-24-20.

14. Margaret Hamburg and Mark Smolinski, "The Coronavirus Outbreak Is a Wake-Up Call Showing How Unprepared We Are to Deal with Biological Threats," *Newsweek*, February 3, 2020, https://www.newsweek. com/coronavirus-outbreak-wake-call-showing-how -unprepared-we-are-deal-biological-threats-1485316.

15. Ed Yong, "The Next Plague Is Coming. Is America Ready?", *The Atlantic*, July/August 2018,

https://www.theatlantic.com/magazine/archive/2018/07/when-the-next-plague-hits/561734/.

16. Laura Spinney, *Pale Rider: The Spanish Flu of 1918 and How It Changed the World* (New York: PublicAffairs, 2017), 187.

17. Mohler, "Coronavirus Spreads in China."

Chapter 7: Surviving a Stampede

1. According to BibleGateway.com, the word *throne* is used thirty-eight times in the New International Version, but that number varies from one Bible translation to the next. Others claim a greater frequency: forty-six times according to Mike Vestel, "The Seven Key Words of Revelation," Polishing the Pulpit, January 23, 2017, https://polishingthepulpit.com/the-seven-key-words -of-revelation/; and forty-seven times according to Justin Taylor, "'Thrones' in Revelation," The Gospel Coalition, October 7, 2009, quoting Sam Storms, https://www.thegospelcoalition.org/blogs/justin-taylor /thrones-in-revelation/.

2. Ben Patterson, *Muscular Faith* (Carol Stream, IL: Salt River, 2011), 176.

3. Martin Luther, "Whether One May Flee from a Deadly Plague," *Luther's Works*, vol. 43: *Devotional Writings II* (Philadelphia: Fortress Press, 1999), as quoted in *The Lutheran Witness*, accessed March 23, 2020, https://blogs.lcms.org/wp-content/uploads/2020/03/Plague -blogLW.pdf.

4. John Sandeman, "'Should a Christian Flee the Plague?'

Martin Luther Was Asked," *Eternity News*, March 13, 2020, https://www.eternitynews.com.au/world/should-a-christian-flee-the-plague-martin-luther-was-asked/.

5. Adapted from Charles R. Swindoll, *Finding God When the World's on Fire* (Franklin, TN: Worthy Inspired, 2016), 8–9.

6. S. D. Gordon, *Quiet Talks on Prayer* (New York: Revell, 1941), 18; some attribute quote to John Bunyan, but source is unknown.

7. Geoff Chang, "5 Lessons from Spurgeon's Ministry in a Cholera Outbreak," The Gospel Coalition, March 17, 2020, https://www.thegospelcoalition.org/article/spurgeon-ministry-cholera-outbreak/.

8. Janet and Geoff Benge, *C. T. Studd: No Retreat* (Seattle, WA: YWAM Publishing, 2005), 92–93.

9. Max Lucado, *Fearless* (Nashville, TN: Thomas Nelson, Inc., 2009), 155, 175–176.

Chapter 8: The Universal Virus . . . and Its Cure

1. Daniel C. Richardson, "Unoriginal Sin," *Christian Century*, June 11, 2014, https://www.christiancentury.org/article/2014-06/unoriginal-sin.

2. Dietrich Bonhoeffer, *Creation and Fall*, Dietrich Bonhoeffer Works, Vol. 3 (Minneapolis: Fortress Press, 1997), 140.

3. "Sin Is a Spiritual Virus, and Christ Is the Cure," *Chicago Tribune*, June 6, 2019, https://www.chicagotribune.com/sns-201905211906-tms-bgrahamctnym-a20190606-20190606-story.html.

NOTES

4. Origin unknown.
5. Walter L. Wilson, *The Romance of a Doctor's Visits* (Chicago: Moody Press, 1935), http://www
.baptistbiblebelievers.com/Books
/TheRomanceoftheDoctorsVisitsWalterWilson.aspx.
6. "Looking for Loopholes," Bible.org, accessed April 2, 2020, https://bible.org/illustration/looking-loopholes.
7. Henry Nouwen, *Writings* (Maryknoll, NY: Orbis Books, 1998), 55.

ABOUT THE AUTHOR

Mark Hitchcock has authored more than thirty books related to Bible prophecy. He has earned ThM and PhD degrees from Dallas Theological Seminary and is an associate professor there. He lives in Edmond, Oklahoma, with his wife, Cheryl, and serves as senior pastor of Faith Bible Church. He and his wife have two married sons and three grandchildren.

Also Available from Mark Hitchcock

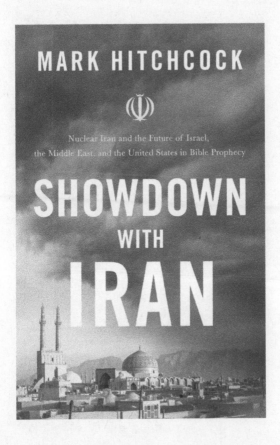

Learn why this nation is historically so dangerous and its role in the future of Israel and the United States. Discover how to be alert, aware, and even hopeful during these changing times!